BUDDHISM:
The Big Picture Explained

BUDDHISM:
THE BIG PICTURE
EXPLAINED
IN COMPARISON
WITH OTHER RELIGIONS

Edward P. H. Woo

iUniverse, Inc.
New York   Bloomington

Buddhism: The Big Picture Explained

Copyright © 2008 by Edward P. H. Woo

All rights reserved. No part of this book may be used or reproduced by any means, graphic, electronic, or mechanical, including photocopying, recording, taping or by any information storage retrieval system without the written permission of the publisher and/ or the author except in the case of brief quotations embodied in critical articles and reviews.

iUniverse books may be ordered through booksellers or by contacting:

iUniverse
1663 Liberty Drive
Bloomington, IN 47403
www.iuniverse.com
1-800-Authors (1-800-288-4677)

Because of the dynamic nature of the Internet, any Web addresses or links contained in this book may have changed since publication and may no longer be valid.

The views expressed in this work are solely those of the author and do not necessarily reflect the views of the publisher, and the publisher hereby disclaims any responsibility for them.

ISBN: 978-0-595-44727-5 (pbk)
ISBN: 978-0-595-69137-1 (cloth)
ISBN: 978-0-595-89048-4 (ebk)

iUniverse Rev Date 12/24/2008
Printed in the United States of America

Contents

Acknowledgments vii
Preface ix
Introduction xiii

Part 1: The Big Picture 1
   1. What Is a Religion? 3
   2. What Is Buddhism? 9
   3. Buddhism and Christianity Compared 16

Part 2: Important Information We Need to Know to Appreciate Buddhism 27
   4. How Does Buddhism Explain the Phenomena We Find in Life? 29
   5. What Is the Real Benefit of Learning Buddhism? 33
   6. A Code of Conduct to Cultivate 39
   7. The Sutras 49
   8. The Four Noble Truths 56
   9. The Eight Rightful Paths 59
  10. How Things Come to Happen 62
  11. The Six Paramitas 67
  12. The Ten Great Vows (Wishes) of Universal Worthy Bodhisattva 70
  13. The Four Stages to Monitor Our Cultivation 75
  14. The Three Important Linkages in Learning 77
  15. The Six Harmonies in Communal Cultivation 79
  16. Emptiness 81
  17. The Three Markings 86
  18. The One Unity Perception 90

Part 3: Reasons for Skepticism and Suspicion about Buddhism 95
  19. Explanation of the Theravada and Mahayana Perspectives 97
  20. Understanding the Rise of Schools of Thought in Buddhism 101
  21. The Problem of Missing the Main Theme of Buddhism 107
  22. The Misconception That Buddhism Is Polytheistic ... 112

Part 4: Looking Ahead from the Buddhist Perspective 119
    23. A Look at the Future 121

Appendix 131

Glossary 134

About the Author 141

Index 143

Acknowledgments

I am deeply grateful to Venerable Master Chin Kung for making the publication of this book possible. First of all, he introduced Buddhist principles to me in such a way that they have changed my outlook on life. Secondly, he advised me of the desirability of imparting the knowledge of Buddhism to the uninformed. Without his encouragement and support in writing this book, I would not have thought of the idea.

I am also grateful for the support of his students including, in particular, Dr. Mao-sen Zhong, who is like a living encyclopedia on anything touching upon Buddhism. Special thanks go to my wife, Monica, and the other members of my family for their understanding and patience.

I would also like to express my appreciation to David Bernardi for his editorial contributions to this book.

I am greatly indebted to his holiness (Professor) Thomas Y. Lin and Crystal Chu Rinpoche who have constantly demonstrated to me the practical application of Buddhist principles to our life and to world affairs.

Preface

I am ethnically Chinese and was brought up in a family with a strong traditional Chinese cultural background. As far as the religious preferences of individual members of the family are concerned, there has always been absolute freedom.

My grandfather was a writer and thinker (1847–1916) who lived during the final years of the T'sing Dynasty. As a dedicated scholar, he wrote on a variety of topics. In my effort to republish his works,[1] I discovered that he had written extensively on a sutra known as the Nirvana Sutra. In his writings, he expressed the view that a balance must be struck between Buddhist teachings and philosophy to produce an ideal society. While I share his views, I have a less ambitious objective. I feel that the world, especially the Western world, seems to have a somewhat distorted idea of what Buddhism is about. On this account, I am convinced that something has to be done to assist Westerners to understand the core values of Buddhist principles. I would like to do this by using this book to explain in simple terms what Buddhism is all about.

I decided to write this book for the following reasons:

1. I am convinced that Buddhist principles are sound.
2. One of the most revered tasks a person can embark upon is to help others to properly evaluate the purpose of life. Hence, I firmly believe that it is the right and proper thing for me to promote Buddhism. I am aware that to help others to understand the purpose of life, in normal circumstances, is even more meaningful than to render to them financial support.
3. I believe that I have the ability to clearly explain the Buddhist principles to Westerners. I am grateful that the circumstances I am in today have made it possible for me to do so.

Therefore, I think I have found a purpose in life—namely, to spend my time and energy during the remainder of my life in promoting Buddhism to the uninformed. This book is an important step in that direction.

---

1   Known as 胡翼南全集. A compilation consisting of eight volumes containing the complete work of Hu Yieh-nan, a set of which is kept at the centre for Research on the history of the T'sing Dynasty, a unit established under the State Councilof the PRC中国国务院清史研究室.

I was trained as a lawyer and worked in private practice as a solicitor in Hong Kong until I retired in 1990.

I am grateful to two people who introduced me to Buddhism. The first is Professor Thomas Lin Yun. Professor Lin is a spectacular figure in the promotion of Buddhism through his leadership as the head of Black Sect Tantric Buddhism, belonging to the Esoteric School of Buddhism. From my observations since I came to know him in 1984, Professor Lin has spent his life doing three things: providing advice and guidance to solve other people's problems, performing "transcendental cures" for those who come to him for help, and teaching Buddhist principles and Chinese culture.

There is never a shortage of people coming to him for help and afterward, praising him and relaying some spectacular success stories from following Professor Lin's advice. I have not a shadow of doubt about the authenticity of these stories. Although no one could say what would have happened if these people did not follow his advice, there is no doubt that Professor Lin is extraordinary. I sometimes wonder if Professor Lin acquired his inexplicable wisdom through his ability to remove greed, hatred, and delusions.

Although he occasionally gives formal lectures, Professor Lin usually teaches in group discussions. He rarely refers to any specific sutras in his discussions, yet he succeeds in building confidence in Buddhism in the minds of everyone he comes across. He is a symbol of liveliness and practical application in Buddhism. Ask him any question, and Professor Lin will not be slow to give you a well-thought-out response to help you solve your problem.

In addition to Professor Lin, another very important figure I have the privilege of knowing who has encouraged and supported me in writing this book is the very well-known venerable master Chin Kung.

Master Chin Kung has probably spent more time than anyone explaining Buddhist principles before the TV camera. He speaks with perfect clarity, and his calligraphy is immaculate. His explanation of the various sutras is invaluable. It is just as helpful for beginners as for anyone doing profound research on Buddhism. In short, Master Chin Kung is a model of dedication.

I mentioned these prominent and admirable personalities in my preface to this book to show how distinguished personalities with totally different backgrounds and totally different lifestyles can help in the promotion of Buddhism in different ways. Their teachings represent two different schools of thought. As mentioned, Professor Lin belongs to Black Sect Tantric Buddhism, while Master Chin Kung belongs to the Pure Land School.

As the teachings of these religious leaders show, both of these schools share the same core values of Buddhism and use the same principles to explain such core values. It is true that they use different methods to achieve their ultimate objective. This is to be expected and is exactly what the Buddha envisaged.

My sincere hope is that the practitioners of different schools will engage in constructive and friendly dialogue and do what they can to show their respect and admiration to the other schools in introducing Buddhism to the world, especially to the Western world. I have confidence that we all agree that the ultimate objective of Buddhism is to teach Buddhist followers to seek perfection.

As we all know, Christian communities also seek perfection. I have a wish that at some point in time in the future, human beings will realize that all religions have the same common goal—the goal of happiness—to be achieved in their pursuit of perfection.

E. P. H. W.

Introduction

Buddhism contains a comprehensive set of ideas on practically everything we see, hear, think about, and come into contact with. Simply put, it seems to have an answer for everything.

How does one summarize the essence of Buddhist teachings? We appreciate that humans have a conscience. Our consciences enable us to distinguish between right and wrong. A distant cousin of conscience is what Buddhist teachings describe as "self-nature."[2] Self-nature is immaculate. Unfortunately, it is blocked by greed, hatred, and delusion. These three poisons, as they are called, have not only blocked our self-nature; often, they also block our consciences. Buddhist teachings tell us that in our lifetimes, we should try to remove that blockage and restore our self-nature.

Essentially, Buddhism explains the above principles, elaborates on what we should do, and explains to us the consequences of our failure to do what we ought to do.

Based upon the teachings of the Buddha,[3] the followers of Buddha produced huge volumes of teaching materials known as *sutras*. Commentaries on these sutras are also available.

Traditionally, Chinese people have always been rather receptive to new ideas. The highest ruling authorities in China throughout the centuries, including specifically Emperors Táng Tài Zōng[4] and Táng Gāo Zōng[5] who reigned during the seventh century, were especially fascinated by the Buddhist concepts. They initiated a gigantic effort to have these voluminous texts translated into Chinese. Through their efforts, future generations of Chinese people had the benefit of being in a position to analyze Buddhism in their own language. It was Emperor Qianlong (1711–1799) of the T'sing Dynasty who commissioned the official publication of what is known as the Qianlong Great Buddhist Canon.[6] It is com-

---

2 自性.

3 The founder of Buddhism was Shakyamuni who lived in India during the sixth century BC. *Shakya* means compassion; *muni* means tranquility and purity. Before his call to religious research, he was a prince known as Siddhartha Gautama.

4 唐太宗.

5 唐高宗.

6 乾隆大藏經.

prised of 120 volumes, which contained all the sutras and commentaries in the Chinese language.

How do the scholars in the Western world acquire knowledge about Buddhism? Unless they do their own research in Sri Lanka, Thailand, Nepal, and other such distant locales, modern scholars will have to rely on the research of other contemporary scholars. These other scholars quote from sources that they think are authentic. But what is authentic and what is not? There is no way to find out other than from the sutras and their commentaries. If one understands Chinese, one would realize that, compared with materials printed in English, there is much more substance available in Chinese from which to seek guidance.

If you read only contemporary books, especially ones written in English, it is easy to miss the big picture. The emphasis is easily misplaced. In many instances, the main focus is slightly deviated, making Buddhism look unnecessarily complicated.

Without proper focus, a person might find it impossible to understand Buddhism, let alone accept it. This book is intended to put the focus right and make it easy for people to understand Buddhism. In this book, I have provided the Chinese versions of many of the terms used in Buddhist teachings as a reference, and I have also quoted from the Chinese version of some of the sutras. Most of these sutras have been in existence since shortly after the time of Buddha. I quote the Chinese source for two reasons: first, to provide greater clarity to those who may happen to understand Chinese, and second, to show that these terms are not an invention of modern-day philosophers.

The book is meant for beginners—those who do not have a clue about Buddhism. Those who think they know about Buddhism could, of course, benefit from it as well. Some readers may want to go deeper in their research on this exciting religion, and they are invited to read the books written by Venerable Master Chin Kung[7] (herein referred to as Master Chin Kung). I mention three books in particular:

1. Understanding Buddhism, a series of lectures by Master Chin Kung,[8]
2. Understanding Buddhism, extracts from teachings by Master Chin Kung,[9] and
3. A compilation of lectures called The Development of Benevolence without Attachment.[10]

---

7   净空法师.
8   认识佛教讲述.（净空法师）
9   认识佛教节录.（净空法师）
10 无住生心集.（净空法师讲述）

I make special reference to the above titles because they have provided the basic source of information for me whenever I am in doubt. For more than the last fifty years, Master Chin Kung has dedicated his life to being a monk and a teacher of Buddhism. He has recorded thousands of hours of lectures covering a wide variety of topics in Buddhist teachings. To give you an idea of the level of detail in the contribution offered by Master Chin Kung, I point to the following example. In the explanation of the sutra known as the Diamond Sutra,[11] which was translated into Chinese during the Tang Dynasty, Master Chin Kung spent one whole year lecturing on a daily basis to explain it.

I confess that my knowledge of Buddhism is superficial. I realize that I am duty bound to present a truthful account, though my presentation might be overly simplistic. Subject to this observation, it is fair to say that it does not take a PhD to write a book for novice students. So although what I say is largely superficial, I hope that I have laid a solid foundation for students serious about learning about Buddhism. A reader can expect to gain a basic knowledge of Buddhism through reading this book. For anyone who wants to know more about Buddhism, we recommend close study of the three books mentioned above. If some readers want to engage in an in-depth study, we recommend they begin by studying the sutra of their choice. I wish to advise that a televised recording of a series of lectures on many sutras, including the Diamond Sutra, is available for free at the Web site given in the footnotes. They are most helpful if you have the patience to watch them.[12]

In writing this book, I have three main goals:

1. To enable those who have very little knowledge about Buddhism to understand what Buddhism is all about.
2. To enable those who are presently following another faith and want to know what Buddhism is about to learn more. (I do not for one moment wish to "convert" anyone to Buddhism.)
3. To explain the "big picture" of Buddhism to those who, for one reason or another, have been led to believe that the principles of Buddhism are bad or inferior compared with those of some other religions with which they are familiar.

I have divided the book into four parts. Part 1 provides an explanation of the main theme of Buddhism. Part 2 provides some important information a person should know to appreciate Buddhism. Part 3 discusses the variety of reasons some

---

11 金刚经.

12 They are available at the Web site of the Dallas Buddhist Association: http://www.amtb-dba.org/English/index.html.

people are hesitant about joining the Buddhist faith. Part 4 looks at the future from a Buddhist perspective. I also discuss the relationship between Buddhist teachings and peace.

A Map to Show the Way

In order to put our readers on the right path for learning Buddhism, I would like to compare this book with a map contained in a tourist guide. This map is complete with legends and notes, showing the location of destinations you may want to visit. Imagine yourself as a tourist using the map, trying to find out how to get to a certain destination. Your destination could be seen as a place across a river.

You can also see your position on the map. Before you can reach the waterfront to cross the river, you must traverse a range of hills and slopes. To provide a guideline for travelers using the map, there will be explanatory notes on the forests, cascades, landscape, terrain, and the danger involved in moving through this territory. The map will also provide advice on what one should do if one encounters difficulty during one's journey.

The core teaching of Buddhism, as stated in Chapter 2, is that there is a destination for every one of us. The restoration of our self-nature is our destination. The inevitable relationship between cause and consequence has shown us that it takes time and effort to reach our destination. There is a process to go through. Whenever we do something bad, we hurt ourselves as a result of our shortsightedness, negligence, oversight, or recklessness, and it prolongs the process of reaching our destination. This is comparable to a person having to experience a rebirth and having to go through the agony of another life or lives. Good deeds will take us a step closer to our destination. Obviously, the trip to the destination may take more than one life.

Chapter 4 explains why some people are more fortunate than others. We can say that the unfortunate people are like those who have fallen down and who have hurt themselves. This is explained by their wrongful behavior during a previous life. If someone has hurt himself, through his greed, hatred, and delusion, it is obvious that he will need to regain his composure and exert a greater effort to resume his journey to his destination.

The real benefit of learning Buddhism (as discussed in Chapter 5) is comparable to the benefit one would get using the map. It certainly helps.

The code of conduct discussed in Chapter 6 is like a piece of advice highlighting a route for you to follow. What is offered is a possible route. However, it may not be the only route.

The discussions in Chapter 11, dealing with the Six Paramitas, serve a similar purpose. They provide another route.

The sutras discussed in Chapter 7 are comparable to reference materials provided to you. You may want to check these materials to give you confidence that you are on the right track.

The Four Noble Truths (discussed in Chapter 8) and the Eight Rightful Paths (discussed in Chapter 9) teach us how to handle different situations. This is like providing you with a compass or a flashlight to make sure that you find your way even when the weather is bad or it is dark.

Yuán Qǐ Fǎ (discussed in Chapter 10), emptiness (discussed in Chapter 16), the Three Markings (discussed in Chapter 17), and the One Unity Perception (discussed in Chapter 18) all deal with certain concepts in Buddhist studies. They are not easy for the novice to appreciate, but they are quite useful in promoting one's understanding of Buddhism. Awareness of these concepts is not an absolute prerequisite to enlightenment, but each serves as a compass or tool to show you the right direction.

The Three Important Linkages (discussed in Chapter 14) are quite useful because they are simple and they help you to achieve results with steady progress. This is like advice that you should rest during the night and walk through the forest when you are fully refreshed in the morning. It helps you to adopt a step-by-step approach.

Chapter 13 deals with the Four Stages to monitor our achievement. These monitors are like markings along a route confirming that you have reached a certain point and to guide you along the way.

After we have learned the big picture of Buddhism, many of us will want to start to do cultivation. The latter part of Chapter 6 provides readers with a simple guideline on the way to proceed.

We have taken pains to make sure that you, the reader, are not confused by the complexity of the very interesting concepts of Buddhism. We try to make sure that you will be able to learn these concepts without having your focus on the main theme blurred.

According to Master Chin Kung, we should distinguish between what Buddhism is (佛学) and how to practice what Buddhism teaches (学佛). This book will touch upon both of these subjects.

Part 1

The Big Picture

1

What Is a Religion?

All religions and all religious principles are the ingenious creations of the human mind. Let us analyze how religions come into being. To do so, we must find out why there is a need for religion.

What does the way the mind of a modern human works have in common with the workings of the minds of his earliest ancestors? It is likely that both of them have some inborn feeling about the need to do what is right and to refrain from doing what is wrong. We would refer to this quality of mind, in both modern humans and our earliest ancestors, as the *conscience*.

The notion of right and wrong might be different in different eras. This difference exists because as our minds develop, we are influenced by culture and tradition. As we grow up, through contact with the people who care for us, we develop criteria of right and wrong. Thus, in the world today, we value monogamy within wedlock. It might not be appropriate to use the same guideline to judge the conduct of our early ancestors. At some point in our histories, even slavery and incest were permitted.

Ancient and modern humans have many common priorities and concerns. Early humans, like modern humans, were conscious that the duration of their lives was limited. Both ancient and modern humans would want to know, for example, how soon life would come to an end, whether life could be extended, and what was going to happen upon death. This uncertainty is, without doubt, a matter of great interest for all.

At some stage, humans began to conceptualize the afterlife, including the idea that one will be faced with the consequences of one's actions in the next life if not in this one. Religious concepts and philosophy began to take shape around this idea.

People living in the past were sometimes frightened by the phenomena that they saw, such as thunder and lightning and natural calamities, and they told stories to explain these phenomena. Some thought that there must be a creator. This was a logical proposition, as in the observable world, nothing could exist without someone creating it. They believed that God, the creator, or some other divinity would naturally want to control everything that he created. When they eventually acquired scientific knowledge that refuted what they had previously believed, their mindset began to change. They would then begin to discard old concepts incompatible with a scientific point of view.

Yet, the notion of God creating heaven and earth is deeply entrenched in the Western consciousness. The concept of God is so predominant that many people think that all must accept it. To them, this must be the way to shape our thoughts. That is to say, we must remind ourselves that God created everything and he is there to monitor the conduct of man.

Yet, there is room for an alternative. Based on logic as we humans understand it, whenever we talk of creating an object, we would likely think of someone putting pieces together to form that object. We should not overlook the possibility that some divine power devised a perfect system as a preliminary step to regulate how all things would evolve. Within this perfect system, all things could come into being, and there is no need for divinity to create objects one by one or to monitor how people behave. Perhaps we creatures of every species live within this grand, perfect system. This is a key Buddhist concept.

Challenging the Definition of Religion

The *Oxford Advanced Learner's English-Chinese Dictionary* (*OALECD*) has defined religion as:

(1) A belief in the existence of a supernatural ruling power, the creator and controller of the universe, who has given to man a spiritual nature which continues to exist after the death of the body; (2) one of the various systems of faith and worship based on such belief.

The great religions of the world—namely Christianity, Islam, and Buddhism—are then given as examples.

This definition, like many others in the West, is underpinned by the notion of the existence of a creator, known as "God," and it presupposes that the creator figure is the controller of the universe and everything in it. Generally, Christian academics accept this definition without any query. As one writer puts it, "Most people would say that religion has something to do with belief in God. God, in turn, is understood to be a Supreme Being who created the world and the creatures in it."[1]

If we accept this definition without qualification, Buddhism cannot be a religion. Buddhists, as we shall see, do not believe in the existence of a supernatural ruling power, a creator, or a controller of the universe. If we insist that Buddhism

---

1   Keown, Damien. 2000. *Buddhism: A Very Short Introduction*. New York: Oxford University Press, p. 3.

is a religion, then we must use a different definition or modify the existing one so that it includes Buddhism.

Prominent professor Ninian Smart proposes a different definition of religion. According to Smart, a set of teachings can be considered a religion if it has the following seven dimensions:

1. practical and ritual,
2. experiential and emotional,
3. narrative and mythic,
4. doctrinal and philosophical,
5. ethical and legal,
6. social and institutional, and
7. material.

If we take the above as a guideline to decide whether a teaching is a religion, Buddhism is a religion (and so is Confucianism). Conspicuously absent from Smart's criteria is the provision of what will happen to us in the afterlife. This, I argue, must be a prerequisite for any teaching to qualify as a religion.

We can also understand how the Chinese see religion by analyzing the word itself. The term *religion* is translated as *zōng jiào*,[2] two characters meaning "source" and "teaching," respectively. According to this translation, religion is a teaching that describes the source of our being.

The particular teachings of the world's religions came about for a variety of reasons, some out of fear and others out of wonder. Our fascination with natural phenomena, resulting in fear and hope, was the source of many religions. Yet, the recognition of the existence of a god is not common to all religions and is not a prerequisite for a set of beliefs to be a religion. This seems to be the basic distinction between the East and the West in the understanding of religion.

The *OALECD* cites Buddhism as an example of a great religion. This is so probably because many Westerners believe that Buddhists also worship a god, or perhaps a multiplicity of gods. This is not the case, as we see in the sutras (the "scriptures" of Buddhism), which do not posit a creator or controller of the universe. For this reason, Master Chin Kung has rightly claimed that Buddhism is not a religion as religion is traditionally defined. If we want to take the common approach that Buddhism, as the word is generally understood, is a religion, we need to look for a definition that will truly cover it.

---

2 宗教.

Religion Versus Philosophy

To find out the true meaning of religion, we first need to study how religions differ from philosophy. *Philosophy* is defined by the *OALECD* as:

> (1) The search for knowledge, especially the nature and meaning of existence, and (2) a system of thought resulting from such a search.

Let us imagine what the world would be like if it could be divided into three scenarios. In scenario 1, we would believe that the spirit does not exist, that human beings do not have a conscience, and that upon the death of a person, everything about that person ends. In such a bizarre scenario, we would certainly place a different emphasis on shaping our behavior; animal instinct would probably dictate our conduct. In scenario 2, we would appreciate that we have a conscience, so we would think of doing what was right and refrain from doing what was wrong. Finally, in scenario 3, we would believe that the spiritual being of a person does not come to an end upon the death of the body, and religion would have a role to play.

One can therefore see that philosophy is a search for knowledge of how human beings should behave considering that we have a conscience but without regard to any speculation on what will happen after the end of life.

It is appropriate to demonstrate the application of philosophy through Confucius's teachings of the Eight Virtues[3] of human beings: "filial piety, fraternity, loyalty, trustworthiness, courtesy, honorability, frugality, and appreciation of what is shameful behavior."[4] These eight virtues form the pillars of Chinese culture. They are highly regarded, and their goodness is praised by all religions. Yet, Confucius's teachings do not refer to what is to happen after death. We learn these virtues not because they are in any way affiliated to or taught by any religion.

Religion, on the other hand, always takes into account the fate of the spirit after one's life has ended. Any religious teaching, of course, spells out how a person should behave in this world, based upon what that religion thinks will happen after life.

So we see the difference between religions and philosophy: Religious teachings claim they know what will happen after our present life ends, and philosophy does not. Armed with this knowledge, religions provide us with ideas on how we should behave during our life on earth. Philosophy also teaches us how to behave,

---

3　八德.
4　孝 悌 忠 信 礼 义 廉 耻.

but the teachings are not based upon a projection of what will happen in the afterlife.

Could we then redefine religion? Let us examine the following alternative:

> Religion is a philosophy or a teaching developed from the belief that the spiritual nature of a person continues to exist after the death of the body and a reward or a punishment would be accorded depending on his or her behavior; and based on such belief, there are certain guidelines devised for people to follow.

This definition will cover Buddhism and Hinduism, as well as Christianity, (Catholic and Protestant), and Islam. Only such a definition will do justice to Buddhism.

Having so defined religions, we can see that in this world, there are two types of religions: the first type, type one, is comprised of those believing in a day of final judgment. Type two refers to those not believing in a day of final judgment. In its place is the mechanism for automatic justice through the existence of a relationship between cause and consequence. Type one includes Roman Catholicism, Protestantism, Judaism, Orthodox Christianity, and Islam. Type two includes Buddhism, Taoism, and Hinduism.

Confucianism is not covered by the definition. It does not project what is to happen after life. Both the authorities and the public in China do not treat Confucianism as a religion. In China today, there is a special bureau under the State Council to supervise the administration of all religious matters within the country. Five authentic religions are recognized. They are Buddhism, Taoism, Roman Catholicism, Protestantism, and Islam. Confucianism is not among them. Consult any Chinese person, and he or she will agree that Confucianism is not a religion, though the reason for such a decision is never the subject matter of a serious debate. In the absence of a clear-cut definition of religion, we can never tell whether the West should look upon Confucianism as a religion.

The suggested definition will give us a true understanding of religion. It will help us solve some very important problems. Whether a particular teaching qualifies as a religion, a philosophy, or a cult is one of these problems. Unless we can say for sure whether Buddhism is a religion, we can hardly start to consider the value of its teachings.

The need to have a correct and specific definition of "religion" is a serious issue of practical importance and immense implications, but the seriousness is not realized by most people. In the Western world, huge sums of money are donated to and controlled by charities. Unless otherwise specifically provided for, one of the ways money designated for charity could be spent is for the "promotion of religious belief." But what is religious belief? If religion is not clearly defined, the courts of law in the Western world or in Hong Kong could never justify whether money spent in the promotion of Buddhism is money spent for a charitable purpose.

When religion is clearly defined, this issue will be solved. Above all, nobody can monopolize the way we look at the events likely to occur after life. With the new definition, we can say that religion is a special type of philosophy available for analysis by all mankind. For some individuals, there may be a need to escape from a particular religion. The test for whether there is such a need is subjective, but there is never a need to escape from learning and understanding *religion* as a philosophy covering the very important field of life and death.

When followers of different religions realize that they have a common aim of reaching the most desired destination after their demise, they stand a much better chance of being able to live in harmony side by side in this global village.

2

What Is Buddhism?

Buddhism encompasses a vast philosophy about the reality of life and the circumstances surrounding life. Like any other religion, as we defined the term, it forecasts what will happen after our present lives have ended. Buddhists are convinced that unless a person goes straight to heaven or hell, a rebirth will take place after death, although in the next life, the person might take the form of an animal or some other being. As discussed in the previous chapter, the inclusion of a belief about what is going to happen after life in a philosophy is a necessary ingredient to determine whether that philosophy can be regarded as a religion. The presence of that belief, in our view, has given Buddhism the status of a religion.

Other religions we know of have also provided for a somewhat similar projection. Confucianism does not provide us with a projection of what is to happen after life. On this account, the writer contends that the teachings of Confucius cannot be properly called a religion. Many will argue that Confucianism was placed in a position similar to Taoism and Buddhism for hundreds of years. Confucianism, Buddhism, and Taoism were referred to as the "three teachings"[1] of China throughout the centuries, not as three *religions*, yet some Western scholars[2] view them as about the same.

Most people in the Christian community have some definite notion of what humans will encounter upon their demise. We will face a trial before God for the way we conducted ourselves during our lifetime. After the trial, we will be sent to heaven, hell, or purgatory, as the case may be. Such believers might ask the following questions. If Buddhists do not believe in God, the creator of the universe, who is there to adjudicate the good and evil of a person? Do humans have a duty to discharge? What is the substitute for the trial? In the following sections, we shall see.

---

1 儒教 for Confucianism, 佛教 for Buddhism, and 道教 for Taoism, respectively.
2 Smith, Huston. 1991. *The World's Religions: Our Great Wisdom Traditions.* New York: Harper Collins.

The Two Main Features of Buddhism

What is Buddhism all about? If we have to use one word to describe the main theme of Buddhism, it must be "enlightenment."[3] If we then ask, "What are we supposed to know to get enlightened?" The answer will bring us to the two outstanding features of Buddhism. If we understand these two features, we begin to see the big picture of Buddhism.

There are many concepts to learn in Buddhism. If we do not have a focus, it is not easy to understand it. When we can identify the main features, there will be a breakthrough, and we will be in a position to compare Buddhism to Christianity. These two features are (1) the *appreciation of the human mind (self-nature)*, and (2) the *inevitable relationship between cause and consequence*.

The Appreciation of the Human Mind (Self-nature)

This is the first important outstanding feature of Buddhism. The appreciation of the human mind is expressed in Chinese in the following way:[4]

míng	clarity or understanding
xīn	the mind
jiàn	to appreciate
xìng	nature; the nature of oneself

Buddhist philosophy states that all sentient beings were originally vested with a "self-nature,"[5] known to be perfect and immaculate. This "self-nature" enables an individual to think like the Buddha.[6] This self-nature and the ability associated with it are blocked by the thoughts that an individual invariably develops upon and after birth, which contaminate his mind. The causes for the blockage are (1) greed,[7] (2) hatred,[8] and (3) delusion.[9] Buddhist philosophy teaches us to try to

---

3 觉悟.
4 明心见性.
5 自性; also known as 本性, 本真, or 真如.
6 A person who has reached enlightenment is known as a "Buddha." In Buddhism, everybody has the opportunity to reach enlightenment. This is done through the removal of greed, hatred, and delusion.
7 贪.
8 嗔.
9 痴.

restore the self-nature. If we succeed in restoring this self-nature, we will become perfect and acquire the status of Buddha. Perfection is our aim. If not for the possibility of restoring this self-nature, we would have nothing to look forward to.

Many critics of Buddhism do not see this point. A well-known opponent of Buddhism, Saint-Hilaire,[10] wrote,

> In Greek philosophy, Socrates and Plato have won imperishable glory by giving to the conception of goodness its real place in the soul of man, in the world, and in God; and the fire they kindled has continued to burn and throw more and more light among us. In Buddhism, on the contrary, not a gleam of this divine flame has shown itself, not a single spark has flashed out; and the sun of intelligence, as Plato calls it, has never enlightened those of the Buddhist world.

Obviously, the author above has not considered the significance of the "self-nature" and its restoration. At the very beginning of the first sermon by Shakyamuni (the Buddha) after his enlightenment, as reported in the sutra known as the Flower Adornment (*Avatamsaka*) Sutra (*huá yán jīng*),[11] he was reported to have said, "All sentient beings are vested with the virtue and wisdom of Buddha, and it was consequential upon us being critical of our perception and our rights not being challenged,[12] and us holding a desire to benefit ourselves at the expense of others[13] that made it impossible to realize."

Similarly, in another sutra known as the Perfect Enlightenment Sutra (*yuán jué jīng*), the Buddha said that all sentient beings (through their possession of self-nature) had originally been Buddha.[14]

This immaculate self-nature is inborn in all sentient beings. But as soon as one's mind is set in motion[15] to insist on one's rights not being challenged, to discriminate between *you* and *me* and *he* and *she*, or to think and act in a selfish manner, this nature is blocked.

---

10 Saint-Hilaire, J. Barthelemy. 2002. *The Buddha and His Religion.* New Delhi: Rupa Co.
11 大方广佛华严经. The sutra was translated during the Tang Dynasty. It specifically said, "「一切众生，皆有如来智能觉性，但以妄想执着所障，不能证得」."
12 执着.
13 妄想.
14 一切众生本来是佛， as reported in 圆觉经.
15 起心动念. What it means is that as soon as one's mind is set in motion to consider something (e.g., whether to extend one's love to someone), there is already discrimination.

The understanding of this self-nature and the possibility of restoring this self-nature is the core of Buddhism.

It is possible to restore this self-nature through eliminating greed, hatred, and delusion. If a person succeeds, that person is enlightened. He will then have complete and perfect understanding of nature and all phenomena of the universe and our lives. He will have acquired the status of a Buddha.[16]

Other sutras have repeatedly emphasized the same concept. When learning Buddhism, one must understand this point.

The purpose of Buddhist teachings is to encourage us to restore our self-nature, "to get enlightened, and thereby to distance ourselves from sufferings and at the same time, secure happiness."[17] What this means is that:

1. Man is vested with a self-nature.
2. This self-nature is blocked as a result of greed, hatred, and delusion, and this blockage produces suffering.
3. The way to remove the suffering is to remove the cause; that is, greed, hatred, and delusion. If we succeed, we will have acquired the status of Buddha and we will fully understand everything. Through such an understanding, we can distance ourselves from our sufferings, and we will, as a result and at the same time, obtain happiness.

His Holiness, the Dalai Lama, has said that the very purpose of life is to seek happiness.[18] The test of happiness is quite subjective. Many people would look upon wealth, fame, and glory as their major source of happiness. Surely, His Holiness has no intention of encouraging us to pursue this kind of happiness. I believe that *happiness*, as a purpose in our lives, must be understood as the incidental result of the removal of suffering through enlightenment.

In many publications on Buddhism available in English, we notice that the "Four Noble Truths" are often described as the essence of Buddhism. Understanding the Four Noble Truths is of course important. Every serious student of Buddhism must know about them, but we should appreciate that it is in the context of the restoration of self-nature that the Four Noble Truths are relevant. Furthermore, while Buddhists do not believe in a being called God, it would be wrong to say

---

16 见性成佛.
17 破迷开悟，离苦得乐.
18 His Holiness, the Dalai Lama, and Howard C. Culter. 1998. *The Art of Happiness*. Kent: Coronet Books, p. 3.

simply, "Buddhism is a religion without God" without providing an explanation of self-nature.

While it is possible to eliminate greed, hatred, and delusion, in our effort to do so, we will probably meet with limited success. We have already described what will happen if we achieve complete success in our effort. Even if we succeed in removing only part of the greed, hatred, and delusion, we will at least partially restore our self-nature. We can easily feel the difference.

Restoring this self-nature will enable us to achieve a form of liberation (referred to as nirvana). Buddhist philosophy also teaches us that we, and only we ourselves, are capable of finding the route to enlightenment. The Buddha can help us to find the path, but we human beings have to tread that path.

Even some very prominent professors so far have not placed much importance on the self-nature of Buddhism. When interviewed by Scott London, Professor Ninian Smart of the University of California, Santa Barbara, said that according to Buddhist teachings, the chief problems of human beings "… were greed, hatred, and delusion." He was right. Yet, Professor Smart did not make reference to the self-nature and the consequences of blocking the self-nature.

Many Buddhist teachers talk of the need to be cautious of our conduct. They say, for example, "We must be compassionate," "We must be sincere when we deal with others," "We must be tolerant," or "Do unto others as you would want them to do unto you," etc. People hearing this might say that what is said is no doubt correct but that they have heard teachings of a similar nature before. Many teachers, related or unrelated to Buddhism, have the ability to compose similar sayings. They ask: What is in Buddhism that is so appealing or so special? The answer is: Only when we understand the self-nature of man, as described above, and the possible return to such self-nature, do we appreciate the very outstanding appeal of Buddhism. This self-nature is similar to the nature of God, as Christians would understand God.

The beauty of the idea of self-nature is that a perfect nature is in and around every one of us, enabling us, if we so desire, to stay close to perfection.

The Inevitable Relationship between Cause and Consequence[19]

Now we come to the second important feature of Buddhism. This is the notion that whatever we do, good or bad, big or trivial, will have some consequence that we will have to face. If you do a good deed, you will be rewarded. If you do a bad one, you will get punished. As part of the effect of this "cause and consequence" relationship, Buddhists believe in the existence of a system of successive "rebirths,"

---

19 因缘果报.

providing for a destination for every being upon the termination of his or her life on earth. The concept of rebirth is found in a sutra (*Zhong Yin-Jin*).[20]

Looking at this concept, some critics say that the Buddhist is "looking to nothing but a reward," that is to say, doing good now in exchange for something good in the future. Buddhist teachings, they would say, effectively make what is meant to be a good deed a mercantile transaction.

At first glance, their accusation appears to have some merit. Yet these critics fail to understand that Buddhist teachings aim at restoring self-nature by steering our minds and activities toward perfection. Perfection, in so far as human character is concerned, is the aim of Buddhism. Perfection, no doubt, is also the aim of Christianity.

The inevitable relationship between cause and consequence is consistent and should be read along with two very important principles of Buddhism explaining how things come to happen. These principles are referred to as *Yuán Qǐ Fǎ* and the Twelve Related Causes and Consequences, mentioned in Chapter 10.

If you appreciate the self-nature of man, its blockage and its restoration, and at the same time understand the inevitable relationship between cause and consequence, you have grasped the essence of Buddhism. If you then do what is necessary to cultivate, you will get enlightened. In the Buddhist world, enlightenment is the highest state of achievement.

This is a very important status. A person who has not yet achieved enlightenment is referred to as a common perplexed individual.

We shall compare the logic of Buddhism with that of Christianity in the next chapter.

---

20 中阴经. See Lin, Yan-jiao. 2000. *A Tour of Chinese Buddhism*. Hebei: Hebei Education Publishers, p. 51.

A Summary of the Basic Understanding of Buddhism

Buddhism is the ingenuous creation of a human mind, namely, that of Shakyamuni. He claimed that he was himself enlightened. He taught people what enlightenment was. Enlightenment denotes a true understanding of all things. With such understanding, suffering would come to an end. If we want to be a follower of Buddhism, we are to learn enlightenment.

As a start to learning enlightenment, we have to know at least two things: one, that there is an inevitable relationship between cause and consequence and two, that with our own effort, we can all get enlightened like Shakyamuni did.

Buddhists believe in a rebirth system. The operation of the relationship of cause and consequence depends on the rebirth system. In this system, we will go to one of the six realms after our bodily life has come to an end. If we succeed in getting enlightened, we can avoid the six realms (in a situation which Buddhists call "nirvana"). To reach enlightenment, it is most important that we avoid that which Buddhists call "the three poisons" known as greed, hatred, and delusion.

The scenario after death in Buddhism is strikingly similar to a person going to hell or heaven and facing a trial at the Final Day of Judgment in Christianity.

Then, in Buddhism, there are sutras (similar to scriptures) teaching us how to behave during our life on earth. In these sutras, many theories were expounded. In the following chapters, some of these theories will be briefly discussed to enable us to better appreciate Buddhism.

3

Buddhism and Christianity Compared

The basic difference between Buddhism and Christianity is that whilst Christianity believes that there is a God who created the universe and everything therein, Buddhism believes that things in the universe originate out of a different model: There is no God, but there is a quality of perfection called "self-nature." Self nature is thought to have designed a set of rules to make up a "system" and based on this system, all things happened.

I touched upon the core difference between Buddhism and Christianity in Chapter 1, when I suggested that divinity could have created a perfect system to regulate how all things were to evolve. In this chapter, I shall examine this idea in some detail.

For the purposes of the present discussions, I mean for "Christianity" to stand in for all religions that believe in the existence of God who created the universe and everything therein and who judges the conduct of human beings.

We human beings aim for perfection. Christians seek this perfection through God. In the Buddhist worldview, there is no God, yet Buddhists also seek perfection—through the restoration of their self-nature. Because self-nature is perfect, and we are taught to aim at restoring our self-nature, Christians and Buddhists share the same aim of reaching perfection. They do, however, differ in some of the ways in which they approach this perfection.

The Nature of God and the Process of Things Coming into Being

For Christianity, God created Heaven and Earth and everything there. For Buddhism, self-nature had the capability to create all things.

In the case of Christianity, it appears that there are the following creations in the following sequence:

(1) First, a system to regulate how things would work out;

(2) Then, the creation of planets in our universe;

(3) Then, the creation of living beings on Earth; and

(4) Then, the creation of human beings.

The reason to suggest that there must be a "system" is this: The planets in our universe rotate around the sun. This situation implies that certain rules, namely, the law of motion and the law of gravity etc., etc., were already in place when the planets were created; otherwise, the planets would not rotate around the sun as they do. Because there were such rules, and undoubtedly many other rules, including the famous formula that $E=mc^2$, we can say that there was a system. Hence, we have a good reason to suggest scenario (1).

Christians then say that human beings and other beings were created. Because these beings lived on the planet Earth, the planet must have been in existence before these beings appeared. Hence, we have scenario (2).

Our scientists advise us that based on scientific proof, other living species had started to live on Earth at least 3.5 billion years before man. Hence, we have scenarios (3) and (4).

The time for the different stages of creation could be billions of years apart. Christianity says that God was the creator in each case.

It seems that logically and for the reasons stated, everybody, both Christians and Buddhists alike, has to accept the four stages of things coming into being in the sequence as mentioned above. It is very important to bear in mind that the process of creation was divisible into two steps: the making of a system as a preliminary step, and the creation of the objects as the final step. Such a division will help us to understand the Buddhists' case. The following paragraphs will elaborate this point.

From the perspective of Buddhism, self-nature was responsible for bringing about all things. The system was the first step created by self-nature. In this system, there are many rules, such as the law of gravity, the law of motion, etc., etc. However, there is included in these rules at least one theory which Buddhists believe in and which Christians do not talk about. This is the theory known as *Yuán Qǐ Fǎ* (YQF). YQF is a theory that everything that happens, happens for some reason. We shall further explain what YQF is in Chapter 10. Suffice it to say here that YQF brought about all the things in scenarios 2, 3, and 4 coming into being.

The system mentioned in scenario 1 above (including all the rules therein) is applicable in eternity. It contains detailed and perfect rules to govern every aspect in every field. The same rules are applied everywhere. The details include, for argument's sake, by way of example, the color of a butterfly, the DNA in our cells, and the solar explosions in the universe. The operation and running of all the galaxies in the universe, including the life and death of all beings therein, could not contradict the rules in this system. When our scientists make what they perceive as a major discovery, such as the splitting of the atom in physics, or a cure for cancer in medicine, or the theory of quantum mechanics, we can only say that they have managed to understand a bit of some of the rules in the perfect system.

In Christianity, God is involved in the running of the universe at all times.

In Buddhism, self-nature created the system. Then the system, through YQF, brings into being and sets in motion everything in scenarios 2, 3, and 4. From then on, everything is automatic. Self-nature is not involved in any emotional encounter with the conduct of the human beings and other beings on Earth.

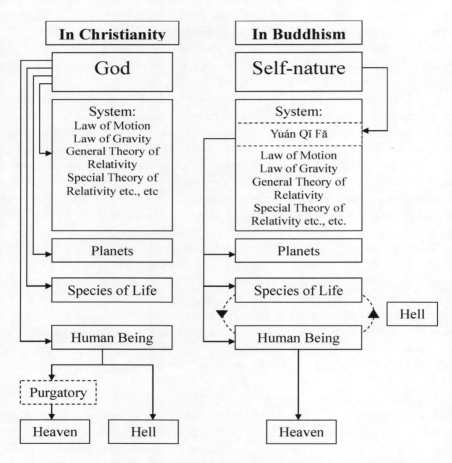

A diagram explaining how things happen according to Christianity and Buddhism

On the left-hand side of this diagram, we see that in Christianity, God created in the following order: (1) a system, (2) the planets, (3) other species of life, and

(4) human beings. After the end of life, a human being will be judged by God and be sent to stay in Heaven or Hell in eternity.

On the right-hand side, we see that in Buddhism, self-nature created a system. This system (specifically through YQF) brought about the existence of the planets and all species of life including human beings. At the end of life, there may be rebirths but, following the system, a human being will ultimately go to Heaven.

This theology could be compared with the thesis proposed by Baruch (later, Benedictus) Spinoza, the seventeenth-century Jewish philosopher who was excommunicated by the Amsterdam synagogue.

Spinoza was known to have rejected the traditional theistic concept of God. Referring to Spinoza, Max Jammer writes, "He denied the traditional theistic concept of God. He denied the existence of a cosmic purpose on the grounds that all events in nature occur according to immutable laws of *cause and effect*. The universe is governed by a mechanical or mathematical order and not according to purposeful or moral intentions."[1]

We can draw a parallel between Spinoza's idea and the Buddhist concept of creation and activities. It seems that Spinoza also believed in the creation of a perfect system in that all things were governed by *cause and effect*. Though he talked of cause and effect, Spinoza probably had no way of knowing and made no reference to the other principles of Buddhism. If Spinoza knew of Buddhism, perhaps he could have explored the possibility of reaching a conclusion understood by and possibly acceptable to Christians and Buddhists alike. There seems to be room for improvement in Spinoza's thesis. Consider the following:

a. After the task of creation envisaged by Spinoza, if God does not take up the role of judging our conduct, God does not appear to have a further role to play. The response from a Buddhist is that God could have produced a system with automatic justice.

b. Some of Spinoza's critics hold the view that if we simply rely on science, such as genes, to explain our conduct, we couldn't even blame Hitler for the atrocities he committed. This argument is valid. Human beings must have the freedom to make their own choices and be held responsible for them. This is what makes life beautiful.

c. There may be perfection in the system Spinoza referred to, but there is not a perfect quality in his God after which we should model ourselves. This point is well taken. However, in the Buddhist world, although there is no God, Buddhists believe in the existence of self-nature. Because self-

---

1   Jammer, Max. 1999. *Einstein and Religion: Physics and Theology.* New Jersey: Princeton University Press, p. 43.

nature is perfect and we are taught to aim at restoring our self-nature, Christians and Buddhists share the same aim of reaching perfection.

Albert Einstein was a great admirer of Spinoza. Referring to him, Einstein said in a poem:

> How much do I love that noble man
> More than I could tell with words
> I fear though he'll remain alone
> With a holy halo of his own.

When Einstein was asked the simple question: Do you believe in God? Einstein replied, "I believe in Spinoza's God who reveals himself in the orderly harmony of what exists, not in a God who concerns himself with fates and actions of human beings."[2]

Beside Spinoza, another important scholar whose thinking about creation made an interesting contribution was Ralph Cudworth, who lived in England in the seventeenth century. Cudworth was a fellow of Emmanuel College. He was master of Clare Hall and later master of Christ's College at Cambridge. What was remarkable was his suggestion that there was a "plastic nature to the universe: God set things in motion, but thereafter the universe behaved according to its own laws."[3] If the universe was taken to mean the planets and all beings therein, naturally including human beings, then Cudworth's thinking was rather consistent with Buddhist philosophy about the causes (or conditions) to bring about events.

I referred to Spinoza and Cudworth and I also quoted Einstein not because they were great thinkers and on that account, they must be right; I quote them because I feel that the principles of Buddhism, like other theological as well as scientific principles, should be examined with an open mind.

When we explore the acceptability of the Buddhist principles, we are investigating a serious proposition. It is a philosophy about life and death and everything we come across. Such a serious proposition must be judged by the acceptability of its logic. Does it appeal to your senses? We are perfectly entitled to use our own judgment to reject anything not considered reasonable. The Buddha is believed to have said, "Don't believe a teaching just because you've heard of it from a man who is supposed to be holy, or because it is contained in a book supposed to be

---

2   Ibid., 49.
3   Winston, Robert. 2005. *The Story of God*. London: Bantam Books, p. 358.

holy, or because all your friends and neighbors believe it. But whatever you have observed and analyzed for yourself and found to be reasonable and good, then accept it and put it into practice."[4]

Religious concepts are open to criticism if they are not consistent with logic or if they do not stand up to the morality of things. The teachings of Buddhism must withstand criticism from the scientific standpoint.

Those who are critical of the creationists' contention may ask: When exactly did God (or self-nature) create the universe, the first human beings, and other beings on earth?

Buddhists essentially say that self-nature brought into being perfect system that has existed since time immemorial. *Yuán* Q F brought about the planets in the universe in its present form. The Buddhists would leave it to the scientists to determine the age of the universe. Indeed, scientists should be encouraged to find out as much as they can about the rules and regulations of this perfect system. Scientific investigations have revealed that human beings have lived on Earth for between three and a half and four million years. Other forms of life lived for three and a half to four billion years before human beings came into existence. Buddhists would not challenge these findings. They are not in the least in conflict with Buddhist concepts.

In answer to the question of when the planets were created, Buddhists would leave the issue to be determined by our scientists. They would not provide an answer arbitrarily. The big bang might be the beginning of our universe, but Buddhists believe that there are other galaxies, the existence of which is now verified by cosmologists. Then, to answer the question of when the first human being was created, Buddhists would also rely upon scientists to provide an answer. Indeed, science and religions should not clash. There is no reason for any feeling of "disenchantment," a term used by many religious researchers. Scientists should be encouraged to figure out as much as they can about the rules of this perfect system.

Ever since Charles Darwin introduced the theory of the survival of the fittest, an ongoing debate has been raging between the religious sector insisting on creation being based on what is known as an intelligent design concept, on the one hand, and the scientists suggesting a process of selection and adaptation on the other. It is interesting that the Buddhist stand is compatible with both the design concept and the concept of evolution: The perfect system is the result of a deliberate design. Selection and adaptation are compatible with YQF. With this observation, I am sure those participating in the debate will have plenty to think about.

---

4   Gach, Gary. 2004. *The Complete Idiot's Guide to Understanding Buddhism (2nd ed)*. New York: Alpha Books, p. 54.

Morality and the Afterlife

Although the beliefs about the mode of the creation of the universe and all creatures therein might be totally different between the two religions, both Christians and Buddhists believe that there should be some means to supervise the conduct of man. In the case of Christianity, God has assumed the role of a judge to adjudicate our conduct. In Buddhism, nobody assumes that role. Justice is in the system. It is the inevitable relationship between cause and consequence that sees to it that all goodness will be rewarded and any evil deed will be punished.

Buddhist followers are taught to aim at perfection. Christians are taught that God is infinitely good and infinitely powerful. We can say Christians believe God is perfect and immaculate in every way. God loves man, and human beings are taught to follow the image of God. They are taught to seek perfection. So, the aim of seeking perfection is a common feature of these two religions.

In Christianity, upon the demise of a person, the deeds that he has done will be judged. As the judge, God will grant to him a place in heaven, hell, or in the case of Roman Catholicism, purgatory.

According to Buddhist philosophy, the deeds carried out by a person will decide whether a person will:

a. Go to the Western World of Supreme Happiness.[5] This is the scenario where Buddhahood is reached, one has acquired nirvana,[6] and self-nature is restored.

b. Undergo a rebirth in one of six realms[7] known as (1) the Heaven Path, (2) the Asura Path, (3) the Human Path, (4) the Creature Path, (5) the Hungry Ghost Path, or (6) hell (also known as Avici Hell[8]), the lowest level of the six realms.

The inevitable relationship between cause and consequence will see to it that this will happen. The end result is strikingly similar between the two religions. Yet, one remarkable distinction between the hell of Christianity and the Avici Hell of Buddhism is that in the former case, a person sent to hell (of Christianity)

---

5   Referred to in Chinese as 西方极乐世界 wherein the four highest rankings of divinity will be accommodated, namely: Buddhas, Bodhisattva, *yuán jué* 缘觉, and *shēng wén* 声闻. They are referred to in Chinese as 四圣法界. Once in this status, they are relieved from the reincarnation cycle.
6   Nirvana is explained in Chapter 17.
7   六道轮回.
8   阿鼻地狱.

will have no hope of reprieve, whilst a person sent to Avici Hell (of Buddhism) will, after he has endured his punishment, still have the chance to do cultivation and will eventually end up experiencing lives in the other realms and finally become a Buddha.

The world is constantly changing and is never static. Let us stretch our imagination to the scenario ten thousand years, one hundred thousand years, or even a million years from today. The species we find must change with the changes in the environment. The climate and temperature might change to such an extent that Earth might no longer be suitable for human habitation. Certain species might cease to exist, and new species might emerge. Human intelligence might not be able to resist the elimination of the human race. Earth might end up without a species called *Homo sapiens*. In such a scenario, the Buddhist system of rebirth would still continue to function. Finally, Earth might be struck with some calamity beyond our imagination, e.g., the evaporation of water and the atmosphere surrounding it. All forms of life might then cease to exist on Earth. Any beings left in Avici Hell will be reprieved. According to what is stated in the Flower Adornment Sutra, every being will have a place in heaven and there will be a Great Perfection.[9] Buddhism is of the view that perfection must be free of suffering. Taking this view, there cannot be perfection in Christianity at the end of time, because there will continue to be suffering in hell lasting through eternity.

Some Observations for Mental Exercise

I believe that as followers of Christianity and Buddhism come to understand each other's positions, they will learn to tolerate each other's thinking, eventually reaching a compromise. Indeed, if we look at the two religions from a new angle, we will see that their differences are rather technical. Please look at the following analysis:

1. Self-nature is equivalent to the nature of Buddha.
2. Self-nature is similar to God's nature in that both are perfect.
3. Self-nature, according to Buddhism, has (through a perfect system) brought about everything in the universe. According to Christian belief, it was God who created the universe and everything in it. Both God and the self-nature are intangible. The two religions give the "creator" a different name.

---

9   情与无情，同成正觉.

4. God judges the conduct of man. But God is infinitely good, infinitely fair, and infinitely efficient. The time it takes for a trial and a judgment to be delivered must be an instant. That is to say, it is automatic in terms of efficiency and fairness. So "the inevitable relationship between cause and consequence" (as in Buddhism) and a judgment by God acting as a judge who is infinitely good, infinitely fair, and infinitely efficient will yield the same result.
5. Both Christianity and Buddhism teach their followers to aim at perfection.
6. The destinations where we go after death are strikingly similar. In one case, it is heaven, hell, or purgatory. In the other case, it is a destination similar to heaven or hell, or in the case of a rebirth, like one having to spend time in purgatory.
7. In many respects, the code of conduct for both religions is similar. The importance of love is emphasized in Christianity, and the importance of compassion in Buddhism.

The mental exercise we recommend you to do is this: Think of the differences and the similarities between Christianity and Buddhism as a start. If you are satisfied that they are similar in the ways we have described, we suggest that you extend your analysis to other religions.

We trust that at the end of the day, you will find a good reason to treat Christianity and Islam as materially the same. Similarly, you might find Hinduism and Buddhism similar. Finally, you might even agree that all are similar.

Should we not, therefore, in the interests of global harmony, ignore the minor discrepancies of different religions and emphasize (perhaps also learn from) the goodness of all religions through their different approaches?

A Summary of the Differences and Similarities between Two Important Religions

	Christianity	Buddhism
The origin of all things	God *What is God?* God is the creator of heaven and earth and everything therein. He supervises all life and everything in the universe he created. He judges our behavior and rewards or punishes us depending on our conduct. We pray to God, and God answers our prayers for help and gives us guidance.	Self-nature *What is self-nature?* It is impossible to define self-nature. We may, however, imagine what it is: Self-nature is a quality perfect and immaculate in every way. It is capable of creating everything. It is a nature inborn in all beings, but self-nature is blocked by greed, hatred, and delusion. Self-nature is responsible for the creation of a system for the universe and everything therein. Everything in the universe evolves around this system. Self-nature does not judge our conduct, and it does not have emotions like love or hatred. It is not an object for worship.
Morality	Man is given discretion to lead his own life. He has a choice either to be good or bad. He needs to be supervised by God, the creator.	Man (as well as all sentient beings) was originally vested with a perfect nature called self-nature. This nature is blocked by his shortcomings in the form of greed, hatred, and delusion acquired during his reincarnation cycle. He needs to be led to the correct path to regain that self-nature. The self-nature is perfect, and it is identical to and is part and parcel of the nature of the Buddha.

	Christianity	**Buddhism**
Creation	1. God has created a perfect system with the law of gravity, law of motion, etc., etc. 2. God has created the universe and everything therein.	1. Self-nature has created a perfect system including the law of gravity, law of motion, etc., but the system has also created Yuán Qǐ Fǎ and an inevitable cause/consequence relationship. 2. Yuán Qǐ Fǎ has brought about everything including the planets and life therein.
The afterlife	At the end of his life, a person faces a trial before God. Depending on his performance, man will be rewarded or punished by a place in heaven or hell or, for a time, in purgatory. In the end of things, there will still be heaven and hell in Christianity.	There is an inevitable relationship between cause and consequence. At the end of his life and at all times, man will be accorded good or bad consequences depending on his deeds. Such deeds include deeds in a past life. The result is automatic, and a trial is unnecessary. Depending on his behavior, an individual will either go straight to heaven or hell or he will be given another chance to lead another life as a human or as some other being. A person sent to Hell still has the chance to join the rebirth cycle and finally go to Heaven.

Part 2

Important Information We Need to Know to Appreciate Buddhism

As the title suggests, the purpose of this book is to explain the big picture. This requires us to take a step back, and at this distance, we may miss the finer details. But how much detail is enough? If we were to accept the simple explanation of Buddhism given in the previous chapter, we would miss out on much of the mysticism and excitement of this fascinating religion. Some of these principles are relatively easy to follow. Others are complex and require much more deliberation to appreciate. In the following chapters, we shall examine a number of interesting topics related to Buddhism. It is my hope that these fine details will entice the reader to take a step closer for a better look.

4

How Does Buddhism Explain the Phenomena We Find in Life?

How does Buddhism explain the phenomena we find in life? For example, why are we rich? Or why are we poor? Why are there good times and bad times in any territory?

From the Buddhists' perspective in examining how things evolve, there are two concepts for consideration: First is the inevitable relationship between cause and consequence. The other is the theory that everything happens for a reason depending on certain causes (or conditions).

Cause and Consequence Relationship[1]

As we have seen in Chapter 2, an absolutely important concept of Buddhism is the belief in the inevitable relationship between cause and consequence. Because of one's conduct in this and possibly in a previous life, something good or terrible might be around the corner. What is reserved for us is sometimes referred to as fate or destiny.

The Causes (or Conditions) to Bring about an Event[2]

This is another important concept. Buddhists believe that quite apart from the principle of the cause and consequence relationship mentioned above, it always takes certain causes or conditions to bring about the happening of any event.

There must be an "initiating cause" to start with. After the initiating cause, there is also a need for some ancillary element called a "triggering cause" to make things happen.

---

1 因缘果报.
2 一切法因缘生.

In order to not get confused, I should mention that the first concept, that is, the cause and consequence concept, is related to morality or ethics and the other concept—the causes (or conditions) to bring about the happening of events—need not be so related. This concept, known as Yuán Qǐ Fǎ, will be discussed further in Chapter 10.

Practical Application of These Two Concepts

Now that we understand these two concepts, we should appreciate that there needs to be a triggering cause to determine what precisely will happen to bring forth any event. So, even if you are originally destined to lead a hard life, what type of hard life and how it is going to take shape you cannot accurately forecast. If you continue to do exceptionally good deeds, you have the chance to postpone the occurrence of the consequence and even avoid facing the fate originally scheduled for you. It is the Buddhists' case that a person's fate can be changed.

The true story of a certain government official in China by the name of Yuán Liǎo-fán[3] who lived during the Ming Dynasty is very revealing in explaining the principle stated above. The story goes that Mr. Yuán had been diagnosed as being destined to lead a mediocre life up to the age of fifty-three when he was to die without being able to get a promotion in his career or to pass the public examination, which was then a prerequisite for advancement. The prediction was so accurate that he found it useless to make an effort to improve himself. He met a very learned monk who taught him about the inevitable relationship between cause and consequence, and he started to do good deeds for a huge number of people. His life suddenly began to improve, and eventually, his fate was completely changed. We can say that the triggering cause was postponed and his fate changed. The story was made into a TV series.[4]

Is the Cause and Consequence Relationship Fair?

I will now come back to the discussion of whether a predetermined arrangement is fair to a person who does not know what has taken place in the past life. The answer is quite simple.

If you believe that your present life is part and parcel of one being experiencing a series of lives, then whether or not you now know what happened in a previous life makes no difference. Buddhism teaches us that we come into existence as a

---

3   袁了凡.

4   Interested readers are invited to obtain a copy from the Web site of Amitabha Buddhist Society, at http://www.amtb-dba.org/English/index.html.

result of a rebirth. Hence, in a sense, it is still the same being. It is, of course, fair for you to face the consequences of your past deeds.

When we come to realize that people appear to have totally different fates beyond their control, for example, some enjoy wealth and glory from their birth, whilst others do not have a moment free of anxiety and suffering, we might ask: Is life really equally fair on everybody? We should appreciate that the Buddhist concept about cause and consequence explains the full story. Life is not only fair; the cause and consequence relationship in Buddhism is the only way to make us feel that life is fair.

So why are we rich? Why are we poor? We are rich not because we are smart. If we are smart, we may be able to make some money, but it does not mean that we can keep it even for a very short time. We can keep our wealth because of something we did in the past. Even if we know how to keep it, some members in the family might do something to deprive us of the chance to keep what we have made.

We may be born with some entrepreneurial genes or some genes which could help us to be very energetic which will make us rich and famous. We may be able to accumulate a huge fortune. Then, we may go too far and become a slave to money. In the end, we may fall into the abyss of greed. Everything is interlinked. The consequence at one stage becomes the cause in the next. There are layers and layers of causes and consequences. Basically, we are rich due to our conduct in a previous life, possibly because in our previous life, we had helped others with our wealth.

> **An Extract from *Understanding Buddhism*, by Master Chin Kung:**
> The Buddha taught us that wealth, wisdom, and long life are all karmic results. If we want to obtain the result, we must first nurture and establish the cause. Good causes result in good results, while bad causes result in bad results or retribution. Where there is a cause, there will be a result and where there is a result, there was a cause. The Buddha taught us that having wealth is the karmic result of a cause planted in former lifetimes. What was this cause? The giving of wealth results in obtaining wealth, the giving of teaching results in obtaining wisdom, the giving of fearlessness results in obtaining health and long life. Therefore, if we wish to have wealth, wisdom, and long and healthy lives in our future, we need to nurture and establish these causes in this lifetime. If we practice the paramita of giving diligently, we will enjoy the benefits and good results in our present lifetime, without needing to wait for the next life. Effect is only created through planting the seed of the cause. This is the law of cause and effect. And this law never changes.[14]

---

5   Master Chin Kung. 2006. *Understanding Buddhism*. Taiwan: The Corporation Republic of Hwa Dzan Society, p. 89.

These two concepts not only determine the plight of individuals; they also determine national as well as world affairs. Let us use the modern history of China to demonstrate the point.

In many respects, events in China during the Cultural Revolution period (1966–1976) exhibited a situation totally unacceptable by any standard. The catastrophic events brought about a complete change of attitude of the members of the ruling Chinese Communist Party, manifested in its meeting in December 1978. At that meeting, the party accepted the proposition that the truth of a theory could only be ascertained from pragmatic experience. It effectively laid down the policy that no philosophy could be looked upon as a foregone conclusion. Wrongful policies must be rectified. If pragmatic experience tells us that a market economy is good for the country, a market economy must be accepted in place of a planned economy. The same argument also applies to private ownership.

The impossible situation during the years of the Cultural Revolution was the cause. This situation called for a change. The change (originally a consequence and now becoming a cause itself) led to prosperity (a new consequence). Looking ahead, we know that prosperity will lead to new problems. The future of China will depend on the decisions made by the authorities from time to time. The fate of a nation is rather similar to the fate of a human being. Everything depends on the decisions of the mind.

The Conclusion

In the final analysis, Buddhism has a clear notion that life is fair. Only through the Buddhist principle of the cause and consequence relationship can we explain why life is equally fair on every one of us.

If we have a reason to think that the world is unfair to us, we will feel unhappy and we might think of doing something which we would not otherwise have dreamt of doing. This is unfortunate. This unfortunate situation is taking place everywhere and every day. It is the cause of jealousy, discontent, confrontation, and conflict, and this is an important area where Buddhism can help.

5

What Is the Real Benefit of Learning Buddhism?

We can say that Buddhism is beneficial (a) to each the individual for personal benefit and (b) for the human species as a whole in the promotion of peace on earth. We shall discuss the benefits of Buddhism under these two separate headings.

The Benefit of Buddhism to the Individual

Buddhism is beneficial to us as individuals because it helps us to understand ourselves[1] and also to understand the environment surrounding us, including the universe. However, to acquire the ultimate benefit, understanding alone is not enough. We need to practice what the sutras have taught us. If we succeed, Buddhists would say that we are enlightened. When we are enlightened, we will find ourselves freed from sufferings.[2]

Even though we might still be a long way from enlightenment, if we appreciate what is happening around us and if we do our cultivation, we will feel contented. Buddhism gives us hope, and it helps us to distance ourselves from wrongdoings. Cultivation is a special term used in Buddhism. It means to do what is expected of a Buddhist to lead a compassionate life free of greed, hatred, and delusion.

We have a reason to pray for help. When we pray to the Buddhas and the Bodhisattvas for help, our prayers will be answered.[3]

So, Buddhism is beneficial for three reasons.

Reason 1: Buddhism helps us understand ourselves and attain enlightenment

Buddhism teaches us to understand that there is a self-nature. The self-nature is capable of creating and did create a perfect system bringing about all sentient

---

1 破迷开悟.
2 离苦得乐.
3 有求必应.

beings and the universe. All sentient beings are equal. The self-nature, which all sentient beings possess, is a demonstration of this equality. We will restore our self-nature when greed, hatred, and delusions are removed. Thus, we learn from Buddhism that there is clearly a purpose in life.

The self-nature was perfect. All sentient beings and everything in the universe are to be treated as one.[4] Evolution is perfectly acceptable to Buddhism. We are taught of the circumstances of our existence, and we know of the inevitable relationship between cause and consequence. We are taught to remember that everything has a reason. We cannot specifically identify the reason today only because our wisdom is blocked by our own shortcomings. If everything we encounter has a reason, there is no point in worrying about our future. Let us do what we can to restore that self-nature and thereby restore our infinite wisdom. This is the first benefit.

Reason 2: Buddhism frees us from suffering

An attempt to cultivate will bring forth the second benefit even though you might still be a long way from enlightenment. The difference between reason 1 and reason 2 is that through reason 1, we are enlightened and of course we find happiness, but through reason 2, we have not yet reached enlightenment, but we already feel contented and happy.

Even with the simple facts of life, Buddhist principles can help us to feel perfectly comfortable and contented. Here is a story of a disgruntled housewife. We can use it as an illustration of the second cited benefit. A situation like the one described here is quite common. We are giving an account of an ordinary housewife in a family living at or near the line of poverty. The story goes that for years, a housewife was used to getting up early in the morning, preparing breakfast for members of her family including her husband, her mother-in-law, and her young child. She had to take her child to school and then return home to do some housework. To help her husband support the family, she also took up a part-time job as a salesperson in multilevel marketing. This had been her way of life for some years. She was content with her situation until one day when she met a former classmate who was married to someone relatively well off. Her friend asked her one question and that changed her outlook: "Why do your family and your husband treat you like a servant?" She began to feel confused. She began to feel perplexed. Discontent began to brew. Tension grew, and her relationship with her husband and her mother-in-law became strained. By chance, she met another classmate who was a Buddhist and who advised her to learn Buddhism.

---

4   Referred to as the One Unity Perception 一合相 in Section 30 of the Diamond Sutra.

She started to read books on Buddhism. After a while, her outlook took a 180-degree turn. She came to know of the need for a person to "give away."[5] This term means "the act and the intent to help others not for any form of reward." Thus, a monetary donation is a form of giving away. Service to others including members of your own family is another form of giving away. For the life of this housewife, materially nothing has changed. The understanding of this simple Buddhist concept has brought her contentment and peace of mind. This example shows how a true understanding can mitigate our suffering.

If you were cheated by someone who at the same time went as far as to slander your character, in normal circumstances, you might want revenge, to fight back and seek redress in a court of law or by some other means. Buddhism teaches us to take a totally different stand. You should realize that you must have done something in your previous life(s), which you now know nothing about. Because of what you did, certain grievances existed between you and the culprit. The culprit thought of a way to get even with you. If you fight back, you will only deepen the grievances. If you can afford to let it go, it would do you good. From the Buddhist point of view, the incident has provided you with an opportunity to cultivate and to express your Bodhi Resolve. This is another example of how Buddhism can help you. There is a saying in Chinese on this point, which is extremely helpful: If you take a step backward, you will find the vastness of the sky and the sea.[6] In other words, in a tense situation, if we are able to forgive or even give up some of our rights, we will likely find that the situation completely changes for our benefit.

Buddhism may help us to feel better in the face of adversity. When we feel frustrated and aggrieved as a result of all kinds of sufferings, such as health, loss of loved ones, pressure at work, failure in exams, or other seemingly insurmountable problems, Buddhist philosophy can provide us with a valid reason for contentment. This is a true relief. Yet, the elimination of the suffering that we encounter during our physical life on earth is only one benefit and not the most important one. The most important one is enlightenment as explained in (1) above, bringing about a state of nirvana.[7]

Reason 3: Buddha always answers our prayers for help

Are prayers always answered? We could ask a Buddhist or a Christian the same question, and we would probably get the same answer. For the sake of argument, we can say that there are four possibilities:

---

5 布施.

6 退一步海阔天空.

7 See Chapter 17 below.

a. I always get what I ask for.
b. I never get what I ask for.
c. Sometimes I get what I ask for.
d. I never feel that my prayer has any effect, and I don't believe that any prayers are ever answered.

If we agree that our prayers are sometimes answered, then it is fair to assume that our prayers are never rejected without a reason. If we did not get a satisfactory response, the reason was either that we were being too greedy or too sinful or we were not repentant enough or not deserving or somehow, we lacked sincerity in our plea.

When a prayer is answered and something we hoped to see has occurred and the occurrence is totally inexplicable, we could describe it as miraculous. We can say that a miracle has happened. A question immediately arises: Do we believe in miracles? There are three ways to explain what we see:

a. We can say that there are miracles.
b. We can refuse to admit that there are miracles. We could just say that something inexplicable has happened. We can refer to it simply as something outside the scope of human intelligence.
c. We can say that it is just a coincidence.

Here is a true story. It may help you appreciate why we believe that the wisdom of human beings is infinite and why something could be done to restore our self-nature and our infinite wisdom.

E and J were two cousins living in an apartment in Vancouver. A third cousin, D, was a medical doctor pursuing postgraduate study on the east coast of Canada. One afternoon, after taking a nap in her apartment, J told E that she had just woken up from a dream. In her dream, D was dead, and she saw his ashes in an urn inside a cubicle onboard a ship. She wanted to go inside the cubicle but was refused admittance. After this conversation, nothing happened until two days later when news came out that D was found dead in his dormitory as result of a rare brain disease. His death had occurred at the time of the dream, although the misfortune did not come to light until two days later when the school authorities realized that D had failed to turn up for classes and started investigating.

The incident was not a miracle. It was not a coincidence. It was something inexplicable. It is beyond human intelligence to know how such a thing could have happened.

The incident was evidence that at that particular moment of time, J had the ability to know something that was totally incomprehensible. She did not know if another such revelation would ever happen again in her lifetime.

Logic tells us that if something can happen once, it can happen again. It is very probable that the ability to tell what is happening three thousand miles away could be developed so that at some point of time in the future, the ability could be available at our fingertips. This incident seems to indicate that if we knew how to develop it, our wisdom could be quite infinite. Buddhists believe that if we succeed in restoring our self-nature, we will have our infinite wisdom restored.

If we pray to Buddha for help, the Buddha could help us to find a way to restore our original infinite wisdom.

The Benefit of Buddhism to Global Peace and Harmony

Buddhism helps to promote peace for at least three reasons:

Reason 1: It removes the "three poisons"

We know that greed, hatred, and delusion (ignorance), sometimes referred to as the "three poisons," are the root causes of all disputes in this world. Buddhism teaches us to abandon these three poisons. Buddhism teaches us to abandon what we are accustomed to claim as a right and learn to cultivate a habit of showing compassion to others.

The political systems around the world are concerned with rights. Democracy has been described as a system of rights. Religions are concerned with love and compassion. Enforcement of rights brings about confrontation. Confrontation turns itself into hatred, and hatred brings about violence. This is not a book on politics, so we will not go too far into analyzing the cause of conflicts. What we want to point out is that in the interests of every one of us, the "rights" of politics must be balanced by the love and compassion demonstrated by religions; otherwise, we will all face the same disastrous consequence.

Reason 2: It teaches us the "One Unity Perception"

The One Unity Perception provides us with a reason to be good to others and to the environment. I will explain this concept in Chapter 18.

Reason 3: It explains to us that we are the masters of our own destiny, and life is fair to every one of us

This aspect has already been discussed in Chapter 4.

6

A Code of Conduct to Cultivate

Buddhism is not abstract. There are specific codes of conduct for man to follow. There are countless ways to do cultivation with a view to achieving enlightenment. Any method capable of achieving a good result in cultivation is referred to as "a Buddha Way." Buddhist teachers call it "Buddha Dharma." When our readers appreciate the core values of Buddhism, they will probably want to know what they should do to log on to the Buddha Way. We will explain what should be done. It is said that there are eighty-four thousand ways to learn Buddhism, but we should not take the figure literally. What we need to appreciate is that there are innumerable routes to achieving the same goal of reaching enlightenment.

Different students in Buddhist studies have different abilities to appreciate what is taught. A method suitable for one may not be suitable for the others. Suppose your teacher tells you that there are five books from which to learn. You browse through these books, and you find that you are still puzzled. Then, you read the books again and again. After a while, you may gradually begin to understand. This is referred to as "gradual appreciation."[1] Your teacher might ask another student to read the same books. This other student might have just begun to look at the cover of the book, and he or she already knows what enlightenment is about. This is called "sudden appreciation."[2]

This difference is not inconsistent as there are myriad ways to learn to enlighten oneself. Indeed, whatever we see might inspire us to suddenly appreciate Buddhist teachings. The Diamond Sutra is very specific in saying that anything could turn out to be a way to teach us Buddhism.[3]

During the reign of the very famous Empress Wu Ze-tian (the only female emperor of China) during the Zhou Dynasty (AD 648–705), as the supreme leader in the country, she ordered the sixth patriarch, Hui-neng, of the Zen School to come to see her at her palace. Patriarch Hui-neng refused to go. She was furious that Patriarch Hui-neng dared to disobey her royal decree, and she was just

---

1 渐悟.
2 顿悟.
3 Section 17 of the Diamond Sutra says that "故如来说：「一切法皆是佛法」."

about to issue the order to punish him when she suddenly realized that the refusal was a Buddha Way to convert her, as it triggered in her a *sudden appreciation* for Buddhism. So, instead of handing down an order for punishment, she directed that awards be generously bestowed on the great Buddhist teacher.

Another person who was reported to have become enlightened was the very famous poet Sū Dōng-pō[4] who lived in China during the Song Dynasty. He came to realize the Buddha Way one day while looking at the greenery of bamboo and the running water flowing along a stream.

Because every way might be a Buddha Way, we can say that Buddhist teaching is quite liberal. It is only to be expected that different schools of thought were developed throughout the centuries. We will discuss the different schools in Chapter 20.

This chapter is a handy guide for the Buddhist student. It is divided into two parts. The first part contains quotations from selected sutras, which describe three levels of attainment. This is the lowest level of Buddhist teaching, in which we are taught to follow certain rules, having a purpose similar to that of the Ten Commandments. The final part of the chapter contains a collection of ideas quoted from the teachings of Master Chin Kung. They are of practical value to any student in the elementary level.

Part 1 – Specific guidance from the sutras for cultivation

For the moment, let us concentrate on one straightforward way to cultivate. In the sutra known as the Visualization Sutra[5] (*Guān Wú Liàng Shòu Jīng*), the Buddha has taught us that a simple way to do cultivation is to follow what is taught in the Three Blessings of Tranquility (or Purity). They relate to three different levels of attainment.

The Three Blessings of Tranquility in Three Levels of Attainment[6]

The Visualization Sutra (*Guān Wú Liàng Shòu Jīng*) dates back to the days of Buddha Shakyamuni. It introduces the Three Blessings of Tranquility, loosely comparable to the Ten Commandments in Christianity. What constitutes the Three Blessings is specific and easy to understand. We shall discuss each of these three blessings.

---

4 苏东坡.
5 观无量寿经.
6 净业三福.

I. The First Blessing of Tranquility (known as the Blessing of Heaven and Man).[7] One has to follow what is taught here whether a student studies in the Theravada or Mahayana perspective.[8] It provides a foundation to learning Buddhism.

II. The Second Blessing of Tranquility (known as the Blessing of the Second Carriage).[9]

III. The Third Blessing of Tranquility (known as the Blessing of the Big Carriage).[10]

It is important that we understand the essence of each of these blessings. They refer to different stages of achievement.

I. The Blessing of Heaven and Man

The first blessing relates to the discharge of our duties and responsibilities. It is similar to teachings in Confucianism, specifically the importance of practicing filial piety and respecting our teachers. This blessing teaches the following:

1. We must show filial piety to our parents.
2. We must respect and serve our teachers.
3. We must remain compassionate and refrain from killing sentient beings (not just human beings but also other forms of living creatures).
4. We must not commit the ten types of wrongs as enumerated. Three of these wrongs originate from our conduct, four from our speech, and the remaining three from our thoughts. To be specific, to govern our conduct,

    (1) we must not kill,

    (2) we must not steal, and

    (3) we must not commit adultery,

    (4) to govern our thoughts, we must stay away from greed,

    (5) hatred, and

7　人天福.
8　More on this in Chapter 19.
9　二乘福.
10　大乘福.

(6) delusion,

(7) to govern our speech, we must not lie,

(8) we must not use abusive language,

(9) we must not make false promises or bear tales, and

(10) we must not use seductive words.

Filial Piety
According to Chinese culture, filial piety is the most important virtue. It is said that filial piety is the first and foremost amongst the virtues of a human being.[11] It is much more than loving one's parents and extending to them financial and other support. Parents are always concerned about the well-being of their children. As their children, we should avoid doing anything which would call for their concern. One is supposed to realize the expectation which parents have of young children growing up as good, law-abiding, and responsible citizens. Thus, one would be considered to have extended filial piety to one's parents only if one lives up to such expectations.

Filial piety is also the first quality a Buddhist student must learn at the most elementary level. Without this quality, there is nothing one could say about success in cultivation.

Some Western writers have commented that on certain matters, Buddhism seems in conflict with Confucian values. Specifically, it is suggested that Buddhism invites sons and daughters to leave the family and renounce the world, whilst Confucianism regards the family as the foundation of society. I respectfully submit that this is hardly the case. Buddhism would never suggest that a young person should leave the family against the wishes of his or her parents. On the contrary, both Confucianism and Buddhism consider filial piety first and foremost amongst the virtues of man.

II. *The Blessing of the Second Carriage*

This blessing deals with the methodology and formalities in learning Buddhism, starting with accepting officially the formality to become a Buddhist follower. This process is not dissimilar to getting baptized in Christianity.

---

11 百行孝为先.

1. The refuge in Buddhism. This refers to the formality of joining Buddhism known as "taking refuge in the Triple Jewels (or Triple Gem)." It includes: (1) taking refuge in Buddha, that is, to be awakened to the reality without delusion; (2) taking refuge in Dharma, meaning to have correct understanding without deviation; and (3) taking refuge in Sangha meaning to achieve purity without pollution. The sixth patriarch of the Zen School used a different name to describe the same process. He referred to it as the Triple Jewels of one's self-nature, teaching us three qualities, namely "refuge to awakening, refuge to correct understanding, and refuge to purity [of mind]."

2. The need to follow the Five Precepts.[12] The first four of these five rules apply to everybody. The fifth rule applies only to those who have undertaken to abide by it; namely, it is applicable to those who want to train to be a monk. The five precepts are:

   i. Do not kill sentient beings;
   ii. Do not steal;
   iii. Do not commit sexual misconduct;
   iv. Don't be untruthful in what you say, and
   v. Do not take alcohol.

3. The need to appear to be honorable[13] in upholding Buddhism.

III. The Blessing of the Big Carriage

The third blessing deals with the state of mind of a person in the final state of cultivation. The Bodhi Resolve, understood as the creation of a desire to be selfless and only to serve others, is especially important. This frame of mind is often referred to as the ultimate goal of Buddhism. The essence of the lesson could be summarized in the firm conviction that we must try to restore our self-nature. To have any hope of restoring our self-nature, we must be selfless in offering help to others and not allow our minds to be concerned with any dharma and events. In other words, we must help others for the sake of helping others. We must not think about the reward for now or for the future. We must not aim at gaining publicity or fame for what we do. The point to remember is that we should not be motivated by anything to be compassion-

---

12 持戒.
13 不犯威仪.

ate, not even by a desire to discharge our duty to do good. The Blessing of the Big Carriage refers to:

1. The creation of a desire to be selfless and only look after the interests of others (This is referred to as the Bodhi Resolve) ;[14]
2. The belief of the inevitable relationship between cause and consequence;[15]
3. The need to read and appreciate the sutras and the teachings of Buddha;[16] and
4. The need to encourage those who seek refuge in Buddhism.[17]

Blessings 1 and 2 were regarded as teachings in the Theravada tradition, while Blessing 3 was known to be in the Mahayana perspective. So, the Three Blessings of Tranquility are a step-by-step approach to learning Buddhism.

The Buddha Conservation Sutra[18] has stated categorically that a student of Buddhism should not aim at proceeding to learn Mahayana Buddhism without first learning Theravada Buddhism.[19] That is to say, a student must learn Blessings 1 and 2 before proceeding to Blessing 3.

It is quite important for those of us living in the twenty-first century to know of this quotation from this sutra of the Buddha. In Chapter 19, I explain the distinction between the Theravada tradition and the Mahayana tradition. Theravada Buddhism has been adopted in the Southeast Asian countries while Mahayana Buddhism is practiced in China and Taiwan. Westerners traditionally seek guidance from practitioners in the Southeast Asian countries. The two traditions have a different focus. From what was said in the Buddha Conservation Sutra, it is clear that the Buddha looked upon the two traditions as teaching their followers at two different levels. Theravada was looked upon as the elementary level. It laid down the necessary foundation for further cultivation. That was why one had to understand the Theravada tradition before moving on to the next level.

Today, if we try to explain the difference to the uninformed, a listener might feel that we are trying to advance some reason we thought out today to justify our argument and thereby to promote Mahayana Buddhism contrary to the inter-

---

14 发菩提心.
15 深信因果.
16 读诵大乘.
17 劝进行者.
18 佛藏经.
19 The exact words used in the sutra were "不先学小乘，后学大乘，非佛弟子."

ests of the Theravada tradition. Since we are using an explanation advanced over 2000 years ago, there can hardly be any room to suggest that we invented it. The revelation was specific. It is a perfect answer to comments by those modern scholars who suggest that Theravada and Mahayana are like the Protestant and the Roman Catholic faiths respectively. We shall return to discuss Theravada and Mahayana perspectives in Chapter 19. What we want to emphasize here is the fact that according to what is clearly stated in a sutra dating back to the date of the Buddha, these two terms apply to two different levels of attainment.

> *In Buddhism, what is the most important attitude to take when we deal with others? Is there a special route to follow to learn Buddhism?*
>
> Master Chin Kung has always explained that the most important attitude in Buddhism is *compassion*. There is no special route. The best way to learn Buddhist teachings is to look for the means that are most appropriate and convenient for you.[20]

Part 2 – A Mindset to Cultivate

The suggestions set out below are some basic advice to someone who, having read this book, feels that Buddhism is worth learning and wants to have some specific guidelines for his or her cultivation. The reader is advised to read what is stated below (as a summary of what can be done) at least one more time after he or she has finished reading the whole book.

1. Understand the basic features of Buddhism.
2. Guard against greed, hatred, and delusion. Make sure that wherever possible, you do not fall into the trap of differentiation, illusion, and insistence on one's position and rights. This is not an easy task. What we must do, at the very least, is to appreciate what is expected of us. A partial success is still a success.
3. Understand the Three Blessings of Tranquility.
4. Understand the Six Paramitas (as explained in Chapter 11).

---

20 慈悲为本，方便为门。

5. Remember that the Buddha has taught us that we should learn from our suffering. Do not seek to lead an extravagant life,[21] but there is nothing wrong with staying reasonably comfortable because we should be mindful that whatever we do, we are setting an example to others. So, if I am a boss, I should do what is expected of a boss to set an example for other bosses. The same observation applies to persons holding high positions in any institution or country.

6. Understand the teaching explained in Section 17 of the Diamond Sutra.[22] Any event we come across may be the Buddha's Dharma that triggers our enlightenment.

7. Appreciate the fact that at different times in your life, you will encounter different challenges; sometimes your life is smooth sailing, but at other times, it is rough sea. You may encounter a varying degree of hardship. You should take the view that whatever you encounter provides you with an opportunity to learn something. This attitude is similar to Confucius's teaching when it says that out of three persons staying together, there is bound to be a person who has something for the others to learn and another one whose conduct the others need to avoid imitating.

8. Be mindful that you are always in an environment whereby you have the opportunity to learn to cultivate. The people you encounter—good or bad—could be looked upon as actors showing you how you should behave. They are all your teachers. You are the only student around.

9. If, for some reason, you are deceived, look upon the deception as a means of testing your ability to stay away from anger, one of the three poisons. During your lifetime, there will be many instances when you see that other people want to take advantage of you. When an ordinary person[23] feels like he or she is being deceived, that person will no doubt get angry. This is not a proper attitude to adopt.

10. Be patient even in the face of insults, as the third of the Six Paramitas has taught us. Thus, you may be very truthful to someone. It is often inexplicable why he or she reciprocates ingratitude for your favors. Yet, the reality is that this person deceived you behind your back, causing you grievous injury. This person might even make false accusations against

---

21 In the sutra known as 佛遗教经, the Buddha has explained that after he passed away, his disciples should use the sutras and suffering as their guidelines. Referred to as 以戒 "即便是汝等大师如我在世，无有异也。"

22 Ibid.

23 凡夫.

you. You may wonder what the justification behind all this is. In all fairness, you might think, how could such a thing have happened? You should look at the occurrence as a means to test your patience. If you understand the inevitable relationship between cause and consequence, you should realize that the wrong presently done to you, or the hardship presently inflicted on you, might well be the consequence of something you had done to somebody in your past life. The culprit you now encounter might be making an effort to get even with you. You should accept the consequence and put an end to the whole episode of revenge and counter-revenge. Our friends holding secular views may think that you are giving too much concession to the party who injured you for some selfish reasons. Buddhism tells us that this is not the proper attitude.

11. In the search for wealth and position, do not take another step toward greed, hatred, and delusion. Having so assured ourselves, there is no objection for us to seek a high position in society or longing for wealth if our aim at the bottom of our hearts is to benefit others. If a person like Bill Gates wants to make another billion dollars to add to his charitable foundation, Buddhist principles would see nothing objectionable in that. Further, by way of example, if I want to promote world peace or some other worthy cause, I know that my family and I must possess a certain degree of financial independence before I can do my job properly. My prayer would probably be answered when I pray that I need help to do my job, even though it means that I have asked for some extra income to sustain a reasonable style of living.

12. If you find your life is full of comfort and success, pause and meditate. We should be thankful for what we have. The purpose of a reasonably good standard of living is to set an example of how a person of that status should behave. Always remember to avoid greed, hatred, and delusion. Buddhism teaches us that what we have and what we enjoy is nothing but illusion. Nothing will stay forever. Circumstances are changing all the time. We must learn the necessity of practicing giving away.

13. Always remember the Buddhist principles and be driven by the following five motivations[24] when dealing with others:
    i. Truthfulness and Sincerity
    ii. Purity

---

24 i) 真诚, ii) 清净, iii) 平等, iv) 正觉, v) 慈悲. It is interesting to note that items ii, iii, and iv were taken from the title of the Life Sutra, known as 佛说大乘无量寿庄严平等觉经. Master Chin Kung added items i and v.

    iii. Equality

    iv. The Right Understanding

    v. Compassion

14. Regarding your attitude toward life, learn to be able to:
    i. Thoroughly see through to the true value of things;
    ii. Abandon your rights and what you have;
    iii. Feel comfortable in spite of such abandonment;
    iv. Appreciate that things happen according to the ever-changing conditions around you, so that it is no use craving things beyond your reach;
    v. Be mindful of the Buddha, and recite the sutras.[25]

15. Constantly practice the paramita of giving away, that is, helping others not for the sake of any return. In doing so, you should not feel attached or be influenced by what you see or what you come across.[26] This is described as the ultimate aim of cultivation. The ultimate aim of cultivation is to learn and practice the Bodhi Resolve; the goal is to reach perfection.

16. Always remember that your life and what you see is like dew and lightning. It will disappear in no time.[27] Upon your demise, nothing that you own will follow you, except your karma, that is., the deeds that you have done, whether they are good or bad.[28]

---

25 i) 看破, ii) 放下, iii) 自在, iv) 随缘, v) 念佛, as adopted by Master Chin Kung.

26 Referred to in the Diamond Sutra as 应无所住而行布施.

27 Described in the Diamond Sutra as 一切有为法，如梦幻泡影，如露亦如电，应作如是观.

28 万般将不去，惟有业随身.

7

The Sutras

What are the sutras? The sutras are teachings by the Buddha, initially given verbally but later compiled and written down by his students. What is the purpose of learning the sutras? Master Chin Kung has responded to this question, saying that the sutras explain to us the reality of everything including ourselves and things surrounding us.[1] The sutras make up the main source of teaching materials for learning Buddhism. As recorded in a sutra known as *fó yí jiāo jīng*,[2] the Buddha (Shakyamuni) was asked what and whom to follow after he passed away. In reply, he said that his followers should use the sutras as a guideline rather than listen to the views of any person claiming to be authoritative.

This piece of advice has far-reaching effects. In following the advice of the Buddha, and especially where Buddhist teaching prohibits differentiation, there should not be an institution claiming authority over others. Thus, the rise of different schools of thought becomes a natural consequence. The existence of different schools may, to those who do not understand the background, look confusing, but the benefit is that no institution, however authoritative it thinks it is, can impose its interpretation of matters beyond scientific proof on the rest of us. Therefore, clashes arising from differences are reduced to a minimum.

Nobody has the time to learn all the sutras[3] because of their length and complexity. We can only learn one or two sutras in some detail. All sutras, however, have many things in common. They aim at teaching us perfection. The Esoteric School refers to this as "the Great Perfection"; other schools refer to it as *zhēn rú zì xìng*,[4] meaning the perfection of our self-nature. Among the sutras we learn, we must not give to any one of them an importance over and above the others. They all come within the realm of perfection. They are equal in all respects. The important factor to consider is: Does it help in your appreciation of Buddhist

---

1 He has used four Chinese characters 诸法实相 to explain the situation.
2 佛遗教经.
3 The famous collection of sutras of Emperor Qian-long of the T'sing Dynasty has 121 volumes in fine print.
4 真如自性. (See footnote in Chapter 2.)

49

teachings? Even though we have already mentioned it before, we must not forget that the Buddha has said that all events are Buddha's way of teaching us to learn to cultivate.

The Buddha taught Buddhism for forty-nine years. His recorded teachings are voluminous. As we shall see later in this book, different followers place different emphasis on the importance of each of these sutras. Here, we shall just identify some of these sutras by name. A famous monk by the name of Táng Xuán Zhu ng[5] made an immense contribution through physically bringing the text of the sutras from India to China and translating them into Chinese. We are grateful to him for the service he rendered to make it so convenient for us to learn the Buddhist principles which were so important in shaping Chinese culture. It is said that a convoy returned to Chiang An in AD 645 and the books, comprised of 657 sutras were carried by twenty horses.[6] It is not appropriate to describe in detail the translation work involved, but we want to note the magnitude of the task to impress upon our readers that perhaps there is more to be found in the Chinese translations than what remains of the original work in Sanskrit.

The more commonly known sutras include the following:

1. The Visualization Sutra (Guān wú liàng shòu jīng):[7] This sutra provided the source of material for teaching us the Three Blessings of Tranquility in three different levels of attainment as mentioned in Chapter 6, the Six Paramitas as mentioned in Chapter 11, the Three Important Linkages as mentioned in Chapter 14, the Six Harmonies as mentioned in Chapter 15, and the Ten Great Vows as mentioned in Chapter 12.

2. The Earth Treasure Sutra (dì zàng jīng),[8] known also as the Original Vow of Earth Treasure Bodhisattva Sutra: This sutra is well-known for its emphasis on teaching filial piety.

3. The Amitabha Sutra (ā mí tuó jīng):[9] This sutra is well-known for its explanation of the causes and circumstances for rebirth in the land of Ultimate Bliss, used by the Pure Land School of thought.

4. The Ten Good Deeds Methods Sutra (shí dà shàn yè jīng)[10]

---

5 Referred to as 唐玄奘, otherwise known as 唐三藏.
6 Yeung, Ceng-wen. 2005. *Basic Knowledge about Buddhism in China*. Beijing: Publishers for Religion and Culture, p. 61–64.
7 观无量寿经.
8 地藏经.
9 阿弥陀经.
10 十善业道经.

5. The Big Eight Appreciations Sutra (bā dà rén jué jīng): This sutra is quite informative for the novice student.
6. The Nirvana Sutra[11] (niè pán jīng): As the title suggests, this sutra explains nirvana. The sutra is also well-known for its explanation of the Four Noble Truths.
7. The Flower Adornment Sutra (huā yán jīng):[12] This sutra is said to be "the mother of all Sutras." Practitioners rely on its principles to cultivate; they use the sutra as a cure for their own personal faults. The Hua Yan School uses this sutra as its main reference material.[13]
8. The Diamond Sutra (jīn gāng bō rě bō luó mì jīng)[14]
9. The Heart Sutra, also referred to as Vajra Prajna Paramita Sutra (xīn jīng)[15]
10. The Dharma Flower Sutra, also referred to as the Lotus Sutra (fǎ huā jīng):[16] This is the main sutra used by the Tian Tai School of Thought (tiān tái zōng).

---

11 涅盘经.
12 华严经.
13 See Chapter 20 below.
14 金刚般若波罗密经.
15 心经.
16 法华经.

A Translation of the Bodhisattva's Big Eight Appreciations Sutra

To give you an impression of what a sutra might cover, we have chosen one known as the Bodhisattva's Big Eight Appreciations Sutra (*bā dà rén jué jīng*)[17] to demonstrate. This sutra is quite short. It has eight parts, which explain the circumstances surrounding life. It teaches us eight reasons we need cultivation.

The First Appreciation[18]

Nothing is permanent in this world.

The security of our land is brittle.

Matters[19] are sadly void in essence.

The five elements we encounter[20] are not part of us.

The very existence of things comes and goes.

It is deceptive and devoid of a central theme.

The mind is the source of all evils.

The appearance provides evidence of sin.

If we can look at things from this perspective,

Gradually, we shall feel detached from life and death.[21]

The Second Appreciation[22]

Avarice is the cause of suffering.

Life and death is tiring,

It all starts from greed.

If we compress our desire,

We will find peace in our minds and bodies.

---

17 八大人觉经.
18 【第一觉悟： 世间无常。国土危脆。四大苦空。五阴无我。生灭变异。虚伪无主。心是恶源。形为罪薮。如是观察。渐离生死。】
19 Including the four elements making up the substances: earth, fire, water, and wind.
20 Including the five constituent elements of all existences: form (色), feeling (受), conception (想), impulse (行), and consciousness (识).
21 Meaning we shall enter into a state of nirvana.
22 【第二觉知：多欲为苦，生死疲劳，从贪欲起。少欲无为；身心自在。】

The Third Appreciation[23]

If we have no limit in our desire,
And keep on seeking material wealth and glory,
We will aggravate our sinful karma.
Bodhisattva cannot approve.
Always feel satisfied with what you have.
Be content in poverty and mindful of the dharma teaching.
Exercise wisdom in handling your affairs.

The Fourth Appreciation[24]

Laziness in our practice will make us fall.
We should always practice diligence.
It will break up our afflictions,
Subdue the four forms of demons,[25]
And keep us away from the confinement of Hell and suffering.

The Fifth Appreciation[26]

Breaking away from the ignorance of life and death,
Is constantly the thought of Bodhisattva.
We need to be well read,
To enhance our wisdom and ability, and
To gain eloquence,
In order that we may teach the truth.
So that all will get enlightened and feel happy.

---

23 【第三觉知： 心无厌足，唯得多求，增长罪恶。菩萨不尔。常念知足。安贫守道。唯慧是业。】

24 【第四觉知：懈怠堕落。常行精进。破烦恼恶。摧伏四魔。出阴界狱。】

25 Including the anxiety demon (烦恼魔), the body demon (五阴身魔), the heavenly demon (天魔), and the death demon (死魔).

26 【第五觉悟： 愚痴生死。菩萨常念。广学多闻。增长智能。成就辩才。教化一切。悉以大乐。】

The Sixth Appreciation[27]

In the midst of poverty and grievances,

It is not easy to avoid facing bad karma.

The Bodhisattva will extend equal compassion to all.

Do not differentiate between

Those who love us and those who hate us.

Do not think of other people's errors, and

Do not hate wicked people.

The Seventh Appreciation[28]

It is wrong to overindulge in human desires.

Although we are human,

We should not contaminate ourselves with worldly pleasure.

Always remember the triple gem,

And the basic needs of life.

Be prepared to sacrifice your daily routine;

Adhere to your ideals and purity.

Whilst the route toward divinity has a long way to go,

We extend compassion to all.

The Eighth Appreciation[29]

In the midst of life and death,

Our being is full of problems and anxiety.

Take the Mahayana vows to assist.

Be willing, on behalf of all sentient beings,

To bear their sufferings so as to,

Enable all sentient beings to receive the ultimate happiness.

---

27 【第六觉知： 贫苦多怨。横结恶缘。菩萨布施。等念怨亲。不念旧恶。不憎恶人。】

28 【第七觉悟： 五欲过患。虽为俗人。不染世乐。常念三衣。瓦钵法器。志愿出家。守道清白。梵行高远。慈悲一切。】

29 【第八觉知： 生死炽然。苦恼无量。发大乘心。普济一切。愿代众生。受无量苦。令诸众生。毕竟大乐。】

Conclusion[30]

These eight appreciations make up
What the enlightened one has in mind.
Practice on the right path with due diligence.
Cultivate compassion and build up wisdom.
Join the vehicle of dharma,
To reach the shores of nirvana.

---

30 【如此八事。乃是诸佛菩萨大人之所觉悟。精进行道。慈悲修慧。乘法身船,至涅盘岸。】

8

The Four Noble Truths[1]

These are the famous teachings on "sufferings" delivered by the Buddha in the sutra called the Nirvana Sutra. Human beings have to face different types of suffering. These include physical suffering as well as mental suffering, which we have to endure during our lifetime. Moreover, there is also suffering arising out of the need to undergo rebirths.

Physical suffering can sometimes be cured by medicine. Mental suffering can only be reduced or eradicated by our ability to appreciate the truth.

The Four Noble Truths teach us one principle. This one principle was originally meant to deal with the suffering we as individual human beings face, but it can also be applied to solving all the various types of suffering including war on earth.

The Fourth Noble Truths refer to four interlinked propositions. They are:

1. Suffering—identifying what went wrong
2. Accumulation—identifying the causes of suffering
3. Termination—putting an end to suffering
4. The Way—finding the way to put an end to suffering

If we follow textbooks, written by authors with Western training in Buddhism, we will usually find the discussions on the Four Noble Truths and the Eight Rightful Paths (as discussed in the next chapter) occupying the most prominent position. Many people tend to think that Buddhism is synonymous with the Four Noble Truths or that the Four Noble Truths. Whilst its importance cannot be underestimated, the Mahayanas probably find it impossible to use it as the main feature to attract people to understand Buddhism.

In the view of the author, the Four Noble Truths are not synonymous with Buddhism. Considering them as the central theme is a long way from the truth.

---

1 四圣谛 described by four characters 苦集灭道 with each character representing one of the Four Truths.

If we ask any person brought up in a Chinese society what Buddhism is all about, the answer we'll get is likely that the main focus of Buddhism is "the inevitable relationship between cause and consequence,"² or "I believe good deeds will bring good luck." Most likely, nobody would be in a position to say anything about the Four Noble Truths, except those who have done some in-depth research on Buddhism.

Those who have read about Buddhism will appreciate the importance of "enlightenment." The self-nature of a person has been mentioned in some of the books on Buddhism, but its significance is often missed. What we want to emphasize here is that Buddhism is definitely more than knowledge of the Four Noble Truths. We are not trying to criticize other writers for placing too heavy an emphasis on the Four Noble Truths. Unfortunately, however, too many readers find it impossible to get ahold of the main theme of Buddhism with the materials published.

We appeal to our readers that when we come across the term "Four Noble Truths," we should realize the following:

First, we know that one of the most outstanding features of Buddhism is the realization that we have to face the consequence of our deeds (the inevitable relationship between cause and consequence).

Second, we know of the existence of self-nature. We know that because of greed, hatred, and delusion, our self-nature was blocked. We also know that by eliminating greed, hatred, and delusion in our minds, we can restore our self-nature. We know that once our self-nature is returned, our wisdom will enable us to understand the truth, and with such understanding, all suffering will disappear. Self-nature is the exact equivalent of the nature of Buddha. We can succeed in restoring our self-nature if we follow the Buddhist teachings.

Third, in the context of the Four Noble Truths, we know what they are:

1. Suffering: In our lives, we cannot avoid the sufferings of birth, age, ill health, death, and other forms of pain and the accompanying sense of loss.
2. Accumulation: Accumulation is knowing where the suffering comes from. Buddhists think that it is greed, hatred, and delusion that cause the blockage of our self-nature, resulting in a failure to understand the reality of things and making us find life unbearable. We appreciate that if we have the wisdom to understand things, we will not find what we encounter unbearable.

---

2   因果报应 or 因缘果报.

3. Termination: We know that the suffering will come to an end with the restoration of our self-nature, as mentioned above, and then we will enter what is known as nirvana.
4. The Way: We know the method whereby the suffering can be eliminated. Our suffering can be alleviated if we reduce the level of our greed, hatred, and delusion. Medicine and scientific knowledge can only help in some cases. The recommendation is to follow the Buddhist teachings including but not limited to the Eight Rightful Paths as discussed. Ultimately, we will find nirvana.

When you hear a teacher mentioning the Four Noble Truths, you know the teacher is talking about the four items as enumerated in the third point above. The idea we want to convey to our readers is that we must first of all understand and remember the overriding importance of the first two points. Our life is full of suffering. The Four Noble Truths teach us to understand the reality of things and reach enlightenment. Having reached enlightenment, our sufferings will come to an end and we shall find happiness.

With a correct understanding of Buddhism and the concept of the Four Noble Truths, let us see how we can handle the problems the world faces today.

The world must identify the sufferings it is facing. If we fail to understand our suffering, we are like a medical doctor starting off with a wrong diagnosis or without one. Medical treatment based upon a wrong diagnosis or without one will lead us to nowhere. Look at the situation in the Middle East, which is now spreading to other areas around the globe. We are made to believe that "terrorism" is the problem we face. No doubt, we are all against terrorism, but it is not the real problem. *Terrorism* is only a term used to describe the impression left on the minds of everybody after certain offenders commit horrible crimes against society. The real cause of the suffering is hatred and crimes generated by hatred or ignorance of what is right and what is wrong, i.e., delusion. Greed could be cited as another factor. What we should do to put an end to terrorism is to remove the greed, the hatred, and the delusion.

A clear understanding of the Four Noble Truths will certainly help to solve the problems the world is facing. Our readers will appreciate that Buddhism has a lot to offer.[3]

---

[3] Reference is made to the Four Noble Truths in a speech the author delivered at a global forum for religion, media, and peace, which can be found in the appendix to this book.

9

The Eight Rightful Paths[1]

Another code of guidelines many people, especially those with Theravada perspectives, like to quote is that of the Eight Rightful Paths. These are the paths leading us toward improvement in our cultivation. The ultimate aim of cultivation is, of course, enlightenment; with enlightenment comes the cessation of suffering. The Eight Rightful Paths are:

1. The Right Understanding: A person's views and understanding must be proper.
2. The Right Resolve: If something is not in accord with propriety, one must not think about doing it.
3. The Right Speech: If something is not in accord with propriety, don't talk about it. Do not make empty promises, and do not gossip.
4. The Right Action: If something is not in accord with propriety, don't do it. Don't do deviant things.
5. The Right Livelihood: One should have a correct lifestyle or way of life.
6. The Right Effort: One should be vigorous in one's practice, always thinking, saying, and doing what is right and not what is improper.
7. The Right Mindfulness: One should not have deviant views. One should not think only of oneself and disregard the interests of others.
8. The Right Meditation: One should abandon one's desires and unwholesome dharmas. Try to avoid being self-centered.

There is nothing very spectacular about the Eight Rightful Paths. There are no surprises. What it says is easily understood and perfectly acceptable to most people. We can accept these teachings at their face value.

---

1   八正道. This refers to teachings found in the sutra called 八正道经.

While our minds are still preoccupied with the proper approach in the way we behave, I would like to turn our attention to another important teaching in Buddhism, and that is known as the Middle Way.

The Middle Way

Buddhism is sometimes referred to as "the religion of the Middle Way." In very simple terms, it is said that Buddhist teachings require us not to be involved in excessive indulgence or deprivation, suggesting that the body should be given what it needs to function optimally and no more. This explanation is rather similar to the theory of the golden means between extremes as promoted by traditional Chinese culture or Confucianism.

After one has done some research on Buddhism, one should notice that the term *Middle Way* also has a more profound meaning, and this is the exciting part of it. It deals with the way we interpret things around us. When we look at some objects, we effectively apply our minds from a subjective point of view to evaluate the objects, that is, what we see. For example, when we see what appears to be a human being walking toward us, our minds could have different responses to the scenario. We might look upon the person as:

> A living creature walking toward us;
>
> A carrier of viruses capable of spreading some contagious diseases approaching us;
>
> A possible terrorist planning an attack;
>
> An office worker on his way home;
>
> A friend wanting to greet us;
>
> A salesman wanting to market his products, etc., etc.

How do we come to a conclusion in each case? We, as human beings, apply our minds to the objects we see. The mind will then take a subjective view and decide what it is. The mind is the factor in determining and evaluating all objects and everything and all events around us.

This analysis is referred to as "Ten thousand dharma, one mind."[2] The mind and dharma will explain all that we come across, but we are taught not to place too much emphasis on either of them independent of the other. On the one hand, the reality of things would help us to open up our minds; on the other hand, our

---

2   Referred to as 万法一心.

minds should have the wisdom to cast a proper subjective view of things. This is known as the Middle Way approach.

We should not forget that Buddhism has taught us that the mind is the source of all evil (and goodness).[3] We can see how the mind works when we either follow or step out of line with the Eight Rightful Paths.

---

3   This is from the seventh line in the first of the Eight Appreciations as stated in the Bodhisattva's Big Eight Appreciations Sutra. See Chapter 7 above.

10

How Things Come to Happen

In Chapter 2, we referred to the inevitable relationship between cause and consequence as one of two essential features of Buddhism. In this chapter, we explain how things come about in the light of such a relationship. Buddhists believe in a concept known as *Yuán Qǐ Fǎ*.[1] Some authors refer to it as the concept of "Dependent Origination." The Lin Jia Sutra has stated that all events are brought about by causations.[2] The concept can be summarized as follows.

The Concept of How Things Come to Happen—*Yuán Qǐ Fǎ*

The things, which happen in the universe, including what we see in this world, and what we encounter in our daily life, would not have happened without a cause. It does not happen by sheer chance. We could identify the causation of an event with two elements: the first is the "initiating cause,"[3] and the other is the "triggering cause"[4] which could be looked upon as the coincidental appearance of a final element to trigger the happening of an event.[5] These two terms are used for want of a better description. This sounds fine in theory. In actual practice, it is quite impossible to pinpoint something and identify it as the real initiating cause, as human beings would do offering evidence in a court of law, for there are endless layers and layers of causes to bring about an event.

In terms of timing, the triggering cause must take place relatively closer to the event as compared with the initiating cause, which might have been in existence for some time.

---

1 缘起法, also known as 缘起论.
2 楞伽经云：「一切法，因缘生。」
3 因.
4 缘 or 助缘
5 The more precise reference in Chinese is 因缘和合 and 因缘果报. 因 = the cause, 缘 = the final element, 果 = the result, and 报 = the coming about.

Without the triggering cause, what precisely was going to happen might not be known though the initiating cause could foretell that something was going to happen along a certain direction.

It should be remembered that not every event involves a reward or a punishment. Thus, for an event taking place such as the big bang, according to Buddhist principles, just as with the happening of any other event, there should be an initiating cause and a triggering cause. On closer scrutiny, it is not difficult to see that this initiating cause and this triggering cause are made up of layers and layers of causes. It is never possible to pinpoint something in isolation and call it the initiating cause. Yuán Qǐ Fǎ has explained how all things happen pursuant to the perfect system.

The triggering cause could also be referred to as a "secondary cause" or a "sustaining cause." It is said that this sustaining cause has to be in place in order that an event may continue to exist.

There is a saying in Buddhist teachings[6] translated as: "The happening of an event is consequential upon certain causes staying together, and the termination of that event is consequential upon such causes dissipating." This comment is often used when making reference to the making and breaking of marriages. A well-known scholar in Buddhist studies, Dr. Shih Jing Yin[7] has explained, when referring to matrimonial disputes, that it is quite impossible to identify the true initiating cause or the triggering cause for the breakup of any marriage.

Some readers might ask: Is there such a thing as fate or destiny? The answer is yes. Then they might ask: If everything is destined by our past conduct (or past life), what is the point of us making an effort to be good in the present life?

The answer is that even if one's fate was originally destined to be bad, the exceptionally good deeds which one carries out during one's lifetime can postpone and, in some cases, alter one's destiny.

In Chapter 4, we told the story of a government official of the Ming Dynasty, a Mr. Yuán Liǎo-fán. Buddhism teaches us that nothing is permanent. War might come. Some natural calamity might fall on us and drastically change our surroundings. Therefore, we should be on the lookout for the chance to do the good deeds expected of us and thereby trigger something good or postpone or eliminate something bad.

I would like to relate a true story I experienced. It explains how unexpected circumstances might trigger the occurrence of some totally unpredictable events.

6 　缘聚而生，缘散而灭。
7 　Dr. Shih Jing Yin is the director of the Centre of Buddhist Studies at the University of Hong Kong.

I had intended to promote education and culture in China. A few years back, I bought a piece of property on the outskirts of Beijing as an investment, and I had completed a campus comprising about five hundred thousand square feet built in five blocks. I spent a rather substantial amount of money. While I did have the intention of promoting culture and education, I had also hoped to make my investment a business success. The aim of promoting education did not materialize because for one reason or another, the right conditions to move ahead never came about.

Then something happened, and it triggered my decision to practice the paramita of giving away. This is also an example of how the triggering event might be something completely unpredictable. I was totally fed up with the dishonesty of a character whom I will simply describe as the CEO of a little-known publicly listed company in Hong Kong. In that capacity, he pretended that the company he worked for was controlled by the family of a well-known philanthropist who lived in Hong Kong and who was also a vice chairman of the People's Consultative Council in the People's Republic of China. I was taken in by such representation. In the hope that I could enter into a joint venture with this group thought to be under the control of the family of this well-known philanthropist, and in the hope that I could participate in a secondary public offering to be issued, I transferred 51 percent of the interest in my investment to this group represented by this CEO in exchange for a promissory note and without requiring it to pay out a single cent in cash. The group was unable to fulfill its promise to pay, and it transpired that the alleged involvement of the family of the philanthropist was false. The CEO went as far as to blatantly misappropriate RMB 9 million (about US$1.2 million) in his custody and at the same time started to make wild allegations to justify his conduct. On behalf of the joint venture company now that he had been given this 51 percent control, he created a bogus liability to pay an offshore company, with which he was involved, a staggering sum in excess of RMB 44 million (about US$5.7 million) in the form of an alleged consultation fee. I was very agitated at one stage. Wasn't this a classical case of fraud? I asked. As a natural reaction, I reported the matter to the local police in China. For reasons unknown to me, the report fell on deaf ears. No one was prosecuted. The character later boasted that he had powerful connections in China. I was just frustrated.

Then, at this point in time and by coincidence, I came into contact with some of the lectures of Master Chin Kung and I was introduced to him. I suddenly found a solution. I found it necessary to completely change my attitude in life, especially toward the culprits. I saw that I must guard against hatred entering into my mind. I came to realize that I should look at the monetary loss and damage inflicted on me as the result of something I must have done in my previous life. I decided to set up a foundation and put my investment, after the deduction of all losses and expenses, into this charity. Such a step would help me to put my frustration and anger aside. I could then, pursuant to advice from Master Chin Kung, use my energy and resources to promote my understanding of Buddhist principles to the uninformed in the Western world. At the end of the day, I can say that what initially looked to be something terrible for my investment has turned out to be something immeasurably good for my cultivation. The value to a person of being in a position to achieve results in explaining Buddhism to a vast number of people is incalculable. If I succeed in doing so through the publication of this book, I should thank the culprits for what they did in indirectly triggering this result. My decision to do what I am presently doing is an example of how we can apply Buddhist principles to help us handle our daily affairs. As for the crimes perceived to have been committed, I should feel completely indifferent to whether the culprits receive their due punishment.

Twelve Related Initial and Associate Causes and Consequences

Buddhist principles not only explain the occurrence of events through *Yuán Qǐ Fǎ* as mentioned above; the process of life and death is also explained. This is based on another principle known as the Twelve Related Causes.[8] This important principle of Buddhism explains that life does not come by coincidence. The scenario leading to the creation and the termination of the life of a human being is explained on a step-by-step basis. In this book, we do not provide an explanation of this principle other than this brief description in very general terms. We feel that it is too complicated for primary students. Those who need to find out more about this principle are kindly referred to the book *The Fourteen Lessons of Buddhism*, which contains fourteen recorded lectures by Master Chin Kung.[9]

Summing Up

Before we leave our discussions of *Yuán Qǐ Fǎ* and the Twelve Related Initial Causes, we must understand why we brought up these topics for discussion. We should appreciate that they are two very important concepts in Buddhism. They explain the existence of all things. They should be read in conjunction with another concept referred to in Chapter 22, where I relate the words of the most

---

8   十二因缘.
9   佛学十四讲讲记. Master Chin Kung. 2003. *Fourteen Lessons of Buddhism*. Taiwan: Hong Kong Buddhist Education Foundation Ltd, p. 127–144.

highly respected Hui-neng, the sixth patriarch of the Zen School, who said (in what is known as the Tan Sutra) that self-nature is capable of creating everything, including all activities and presumably also including the perfect system mentioned in Chapter 1.

These two concepts and this perfect system, the author argues, is the way Buddhists explain life and everything in the universe.

11

The Six Paramitas[1]

Many of the sutras refer extensively to the Six Paramitas. One may look at them as a summary of good conduct based upon Buddhist principles. They embrace all that is expected of a person in his attempt to cultivate. A person has to pay attention and practice these paramitas.

Paramita 1: Giving Away

This includes the giving of money and services.[2] There are three types of giving away:[3]

1. Money or assets, including donating money for charitable purposes. Rendering service is also a form of giving away.
2. Knowledge, making people understand the truth of matters, such as Buddhist teachings. This type of giving away has more merit to the giver than monetary donations. In Chapter 2, we mentioned how our self-nature was blocked by greed, hatred, and delusion. Giving will, to a certain extent, offset our greed.
3. Assurance, pacifying fear and calming down the minds of others.

Paramita 2: Abiding by the Precepts[4]

A Buddhist follower is taught to be law-abiding. The precepts provide guidance to perfect conduct and to eliminating evil deeds.

---

1 六度 or 六波罗密. They include 1. 布施; 2. 持戒; 3. 忍辱; 4. 精进; 5. 禅定; 6. 般若.
2 布施.
3 财布施, 法布施, and 无畏布施.
4 持戒.

Paramita 3: Being Patient[5]

The term used in Chinese is slightly different from the English word *patient*. It denotes patience and forbearance in the face of insults. Adopting this attitude will likely result in reducing the hatred within your body, taking you a step closer to the restoration of your self-nature.

In the face of insult, a Buddhist should not succumb to hatred. This is by no means an easy task.

Paramita 4: Vigor

Through specialization and a desire to advance, you should maintain a driving force and sufficient energy in the pursuit of good work.[6]

Paramita 5: Deep Concentration

This is referred to by the two Chinese characters *chán dìng*. Some call it meditational concentration.[7]

Meditation has always been looked upon as an important practice of Buddhists, especially in the Zen School of Buddhism. In fact, all the various schools of thought practice meditation. They refer to the process by different names. The sixth patriarch, Hui-neng, of the Zen School defined meditational concentration in the Platform Sutra (known also as the Tan Sutra).[8]

Chán is defined there as "not attached to one's outward appearance." *Dìng* is defined as "a steady mind unmoved by external factors." Practicing *Chán Dìng* simply means that we are not influenced by external factors and we have a definite purpose in our lives. We can explain it by saying that in whatever we do, we will stick to the purpose of restoring our self-nature.

This is somewhat different from the general notion that we should spend time doing meditation sitting cross-legged in a quiet environment. We say this not because we want to undermine the importance of meditation, as the word is generally understood, but only to explain that the term, as one of the Six Paramitas, has, according to Patriarch Hui-neng, a relatively more specific meaning.

---

5 忍辱.
6 精进.
7 禅定.
8 Known in Chinese as 六祖坛经.

While still on the subject of meditation, we should take note of the fact that, as mentioned above, meditation occupies an important position in Chinese culture. It is stated in a very famous book called *The Big Learning*[9] that:

> Only in stability do we find quietude;
>
> Only in quietude do we find peace of mind;
>
> Only with peace of mind do we produce the capacity to think; and
>
> Only when we have the capacity to think can we achieve our objective.

Paramita 6: Acquiring Wisdom

This is the ability to understand the nature of all things and how they are related to the end.[10] The paramita of wisdom is deeper than wisdom in the ordinary sense of the word in that it includes the ability to appreciate and understand things from the Buddha's point of view. There is nothing that you know, for you have no wandering thoughts, and yet, there is nothing that you don't know.

> The Six Paramitas start with a heart of compassion. We realize that everything has its own methods and continuity. This is abiding by the precepts. With endurance and perseverance, we will have patience. To specialize without slacking is diligence. To be master of our mind and not to be swayed by external conditions is concentration. To thoroughly understand all the phenomena is wisdom. The Buddha has taught us to adopt the Six Paramitas of giving, abiding by the precepts, patience, diligence, deep concentration, and wisdom into our daily lives.
>
> —Master Chin Kung

9　大学.
10　般若.

12

The Ten Great Vows (Wishes) of Universal Worthy Bodhisattva[1]

The Ten Great Vows tell us how to adjust our frame of mind when we enter into the final stages of cultivation toward enlightenment. Let us recap what we have covered. The Flower Adornment Sutra is very specific about what we should do to get results in our effort to cultivate. It teaches us that after following the advice on how we should behave as stated in (1) The Three Blessings,[2] (2) the Six Harmonies,[3] (3) the Three Modes of Learning,[4] and (4) the Six Paramitas,[5] there is still a higher level to enter. This is the Ten Great Vows of Universal Worthy Bodhisattva.

In this book, we will just mention what these vows are about. We could look upon them as advice to graduate students as they take the final steps toward achieving Buddhahood. These vows are not complicated. We will just briefly discuss some of the items, which we think our readers might find of interest.

Those readers who want to carry out additional research on the topic are kindly recommended to access the Web site of the Dallas Buddhist Association for reference.[6]

The Ten Great Vows are:

1. To pay respect to all Buddhas
2. To praise the "Thus Come One"
3. To make offerings extensively

---

1 十大願王.
2 As explained in Chapter 6.
3 As explained in Chapter 15.
4 As explained in Chapter 14.
5 As explained in Chapter 11.
6 http://www.amtb-dba.org/English/index.html

4. To regret karmic obstacles
5. To be joyful over others' meritorious deeds
6. To appeal to the Buddha to turn the Dharma Wheel
7. To request the Buddha to reside in this world
8. To be diligent and consistent as a follower of the Buddha's teachings
9. To be in accord with all sentient beings
10. To dedicate all merits

To Pay Respect to All Buddhas
Please note that in the context of the first vow of the Ten Great Vows, the term *Buddha* has a meaning wider than what the word is generally understood to mean. It covers all beings, sentient or otherwise. In other words, we should extend our respect to everything we encounter. This applies to every sentient being we happen to meet, every object we come across, and every duty we need to discharge. We should show respect even to wicked people. Perfection is our target, and perfection can be achieved only if we pay respect to everything we encounter.

To Praise the "Thus Come One"
The Buddha we praise, as mentioned in the second vow, refers to the Buddha Shakyamuni. Note the difference between paying respect to all beings and praising the Buddha. We pay respect to all beings including wicked people, but we praise only the Buddha.

To Make Offerings Extensively
Offerings here are not confined to making gifts or donations to the temples or other charitable institutions. They refer to the need to appreciate the goodness of practicing giving away. Of the different forms of giving away, it is said that the most important one is our effort to help others to break away from ignorance and to understand the truth. Buddhist students are taught to be generous in this regard.

To Regret Karmic Obstacles
Regretting karmic obstacles refers to a state of mind. Sincerity is the key. Buddhism does not call upon a person to observe any ritual for repentance.

To Be Joyful over Others' Meritorious Deeds
It is not easy to be joyful over the meritorious deeds of others. We need to overcome jealousy. We are not sure if jealousy is regarded as a sin in Christianity, but it is obviously a long way from perfection.

To Appeal to the Buddha to Turn the Dharma Wheel
We should take note of the fact that in ancient days, there were no printing facilities. The text of the sutras was usually written on a scroll mounted on a wheel. The wheel is referred to as the Dharma Wheel. Turning the wheel would enable people to read the text of the scroll. If we turned the wheel 360 degrees, we would have the opportunity to read the entire text written on the scroll once. When we appeal to the Buddha to turn the Dharma Wheel, we remind ourselves of the need to invite qualified persons to explain to us the meaning of Buddhist principles, specifically the sutras.

To Request the Buddha to Reside in This World
This reminds us of the need to find good teachers to explain to us the Buddhist principles.

To Be Diligent in Following Buddha's Teachings
This refers to the need to follow what is taught in the sutras. Only in the sutras can we find the true meaning of Buddhism.

To Accord with All Sentient Beings
When we try to promote Buddhist philosophy to others, we have to make sure that we do what is appropriate. For example, we are advised not to argue with our students to bring our points across.

To Dedicate All Merits
In Buddhism, it is possible to transfer merits. The overriding principle behind such transfer is the Bodhi Resolve. The idea is that by reason of our kindheartedness toward others, whatever merit we have, we should not keep it to ourselves, but rather give it to all sentient beings everywhere. This idea is the essence of Mahayana Buddhism. I recall reading a book on Buddhism written in English mentioning the Buddhist concept about the transfer of merits. It did not explain why there was a system for the transfer of merits. People are bound to inquire: Are we not reducing merits into money in a bank or chips on a gaming table? How could they be transferred? We should appreciate that they are transferred out of

ourselves in order to show our Bodhi Resolve, not to enable us to show favor to "X" in preference to "Y."

Let us see how we can apply the Ten Great Vows in the way we show respect to our ancestors. Suppose my grandfather was known to be a notorious figure, such as a war criminal executed by an international tribunal. Am I supposed to show my respect to him? And what sort of attitude should I tell my children to adopt concerning their great-grandfather? I can see that there are several alternatives:

a. Even though in all truthfulness, I know that my grandfather was guilty of the crime as charged, I could still insist on his innocence and disregard the trial and conviction. As a result of my insistence, some people in the country might, rightly or wrongly, respect me for my blind patriotism. But praising him for his loyalty to his country while ignoring the brutal crimes he committed against humanity is clearly hypocritical and sending the wrong signal to my children.

b. I could insist on his innocence if I genuinely believe that he was wrongly convicted. In such a case, I could pay my respects to him as though the trial and conviction were nonevents.

c. Unless I take the stand stated in (b), I shouldn't mind being sincere and telling my children how I feel. I should make it clear that patriotism is something we all respect, but it is wrong to use it as an excuse to commit brutal crimes against humanity. In this situation, I could still pay my respects to my deceased grandfather based on the explanation of the first vow as outlined above. I could transfer the merits of my karma to him, as mentioned in the tenth vow, in the hope that he will soon be able to be reprieved. I know that in due course, my grandfather might reenter the rebirth cycle and even gain Buddhahood. This attitude would be helpful to my grandfather as well as to his children in all future generations.

d. I could pay my respects to my grandfather and say nothing. Some people might think that adopting this course is diplomatic. Those who know how to analyze the situation will know that I am sending the wrong signal because people will think that I am adopting attitude (a). In fact, I am just being too timid to be specific about my stand.

e. I could refrain from showing respect to my grandfather and say nothing to explain my position. Before I decide not to pay him respect, maybe I should carefully consider my stand. Showing respect to one's ancestors is an important part of Oriental culture. If I fail to show respect to my parents and grandparents, it might be taken as an indication that either

I don't respect the culture or I don't know how to handle the situation in front of my children.

Alternative (b) might or might not be the correct step to take, depending on the circumstances. If this alternative is not taken, I am sure I should take alternative (c). Everyone will respect me for my courage in taking such a step.

Hopefully, with some skill, some sincerity, and some knowledge of Buddhist principles, the knot between Japan and her former enemies over visits to the Yasukuni Shrine[7] can be untied. This is another instance where we can see how Buddhism can help us to solve the problems we face.

---

7   靖国神社.

13

The Four Stages to Monitor Our Cultivation

In learning Buddhism, not only should we learn the Buddhist philosophy, we must also learn to practice cultivation and understand the various stages of our achievements during our cultivation. We can see that there are four different stages in our progress: *belief, understanding, action,* and *verification*.[1] These four stages are referred to in the Flower Adornment Sutra.

Belief

The belief referred to in Buddhism is different from the belief referred to in Christianity. Buddhism does not demand that its followers believe in any supernatural power. A belief in the existence of the inevitable relationship between cause and consequence is, of course a prerequisite. The relationship between cause and consequence is so fundamental that asking people to believe in it is like asking a person to believe that he has a conscience. Apart from this, Buddhism only asks people to have confidence in themselves. Man should realize (and this is another belief that Buddhism has insisted upon) that man himself was originally vested with a self-nature, which was immaculate. It is impossible to prove the existence of self-nature. A certain degree of trust is needed. This self-nature is blocked by one's own shortcomings. If we can succeed in removing these shortcomings, our self-nature can be restored.

Understanding

The most basic understanding that all human beings have is the ability to distinguish between what is right and wrong. Buddhist principles are slightly more

---

1   信解行证.

profound. We must understand the reality of life, of what we are in relation to the universe. Buddhist teachings have provided us with a clear and specific analysis.

Action

Once we have the belief and the true understanding, we can begin to put what we have learned into practice. What we would do is build on our understanding of what we think is appropriate always remembering the need to show compassion.

Verification

This is a roundup of our achievements. When we have confidence in our own capabilities, we will understand what our duties are. We should then do what we think we ought to do. The verification part is important because what we do pursuant to what we think we should do should be a reflection of what we have learned from the sutras.

Writing this book to inform curious individuals about the big picture of Buddhism exemplifies the *action* expected of me once I realized I had the ability to promote the Buddhist principles. If my readers feel they have benefited from the book, then there is *verification*.

14

The Three Important Linkages[1] in Learning

Another concept one has to bear in mind in learning Buddhism is that of the Three Linkages, three important aspects in learning the Buddhist principles. Also known as the "Three Learnings" and the "Three Baskets," these aspects of Buddhist teaching are widely referred to and may serve as an entry point or a point of emphasis in learning Buddhism.

1. **Precepts**—Also known as *rules and regulations, the law, the learning of self-discipline,* or *knowing and appreciating the need for complying with the law.* Knowing the precepts is important. One has to comply with the law and regulations of a territory before one can feel oneself free of fear. Only when one is in such a state of mind can one expect to see things clearly and to make decisions with all due wisdom.
2. **Deep Concentration**—Also known as *acquiring stability* or *peace of mind.* Stability is a state of mind, and it is usually acquired through meditation.
3. **Wisdom**—Wisdom is inborn. One feels it as one eliminates greed, hatred, and delusion.

The following is an extract from *Understanding Buddhism* by Master Chin Kung:

> If we can abide by the precepts and laws, we will have a tranquil body and mind, which will allow us to be free from worries and fear. Deep concentration arises from tranquility. Therefore, the precepts are essential to self-cultivation. If we break the law or the precepts, then our conscience will be plagued by guilt even if no punishment is meted

---

[1] 戒定慧. 戒 = the precepts; 定 = stability, tranquility; and 慧 = wisdom. In Sanskrit, the Three Linkages are referred to as the Tripitaka.

out. When our body and mind are disturbed, we cannot concentrate on our practice. To practice successfully, we need to be tranquil. It is said, "Precepts or self-discipline lead to deep concentration, from which wisdom arises."

If someone is serious about learning Buddhism, it is recommended that this person learn to recite at least one sutra—a short one will do. It is suggested that any one sutra will serve the purpose because all sutras point to restoring our self-nature. Master Chin Kung has suggested that by reciting a sutra, the Three Learnings of self-discipline, deep concentration, and wisdom are achieved at the same time.

Practicing the Three Learnings Concurrently

What is the first step in learning Buddhism in a serious way? Master Chin Kung has advised us to start by reciting one sutra. Self-discipline requires that we "do nothing that is bad." Sutras are words flowing from the Buddha's true nature. Nothing can surpass these words in terms of virtue. Therefore, reciting a sutra is doing all that is good.

When reciting a sutra, we must focus to cultivate concentration. So we have also dealt with concentration. Clear and correct enunciation of every word without any omission is a practice of wisdom.

15

The Six Harmonies in Communal Cultivation[1]

There are certain specific recommendations made with respect to people wanting to do cultivation in a communal environment. These recommendations (or rules) are contained in the sutra known as the Visualization Sutra (*Guān wú liáng shòu jīng*). They were laid down for the purposes of ensuring harmony when a group of four or more persons engage in a communal environment to do cultivation. They are:

1. Consensus in one's approach in dealing with a situation
2. Observing the same set of rules
3. Living together under similar conditions
4. Refraining from lashing out with verbal criticism
5. Sharing the same inner peace and happiness from practicing the teachings
6. Sharing the same benefits harmoniously

Consensus in One's Approach in Dealing with a Situation
A venture cannot succeed if people staying together have different approaches in dealing with a situation. In the context of communal cultivation, without doubt, the goal of the participants is to seek enlightenment. It is essential that they have a common approach to handling the situation. In Chapter 20, we shall discuss how there are different schools of thought in Buddhism. It is not possible to achieve satisfactory results if the participants in communal cultivation adhere to the theories of different schools.

---

1 六和敬. 1. 见和同解 2. 戒和同修 3. 身和同住 4. 口和同住 5. 意和同悦 6. 利和同均. Some teachers like to arrange the Six Harmonies in a different sequence, namely 3, 4, 5, 2, 1, 6 to denote 身, 口, 意, 戒, 见, 利. Such an arrangement will make it easier for a student to remember them.

Observing the Same Set of Rules
When we live and practice together, we need to have rules and regulations because without them, there will be disorder. The rules must be fair, and they must apply to all. These rules need to include the five fundamental precepts set by the Buddha.

Living Together Under Similar Conditions
The purpose of encouraging people to stay together is to create an atmosphere of harmony and for the promotion of community awareness. It is not suggested that anyone should use the monasteries and temples as a means of escape.

Refraining from Lashing Out with Verbal Criticism
All the members who live together need to do so without quarrelling. In this way, they can best concentrate their efforts on cultivation. When people are together, the most frequent act is that of speech, so speech karma is the easiest to commit.

Sharing the Same Inner Peace and Happiness from Practicing the Teachings
This is to savor the dharma joy. Whichever practice method we choose, the basic achievement we have in our practice is happiness. If we feel unhappy after beginning our practice, we have definitely encountered a serious problem, and we must think of a way to solve the problem.

Sharing the Same Benefits Harmoniously
This will be achieved only if we can share all benefits equally. Everyone must ensure that there will be fairness in all things. It is hardly necessary to emphasize the need to avoid greed, anger, and delusion.

16

Emptiness

Emptiness is a term widely used in Buddhist teachings. Buddhist theologians have come up with a variety of interpretations. One source[1] explains:

> Emptiness means that all dharma have no independent existence of their own, apart from the reliance on other dharma. All dharma have no real, individual essences that distinguish them from all other dharma. In other words, everything in the world, both physical and mental, is interdependent with everything else in the world. The temporary existence of each is dependent on its relations with what is not. There is no such thing as something existing on its own, separate and with no causal relation with anything else.

This is probably the standard, classic, and most widely accepted explanation of "emptiness." Emptiness is closely associated with self-nature. Whether things are capable or not capable of individual existence is a separate issue. It is still difficult for beginners to understand how it helps to explain emptiness.

We will try to take a more simplistic approach. When we look at two bowls, we may say one is full and the other empty. This is emptiness in the ordinary sense of the word.

When we look at something (an object), we have a natural tendency to identify what we see with certain qualities closely linked to the object. When we see expensive cars and a display of expensive jewelry, the thought of wealth and luxury comes to mind. When we encounter something unusual, for example someone in our hometown winning a gold medal in the Olympics, a thought such as jubilance enters our minds. Similarly, we cannot escape a thought of sorrow when we hear that a good friend has passed away as a result of injuries received in a traffic accident. According to Buddhist teachings, when we see the dharma (events), we should train ourselves to associate them with emptiness.

---

[1] Epstein, Ronald B. 2003. *Buddhism A to Z*. Taiwan: Editorial Committee of the Buddhist Text Translation Society, p. 71.

A very famous quotation from the Heart Sutra[2] making reference to emptiness can be translated as follows:

> A sight (translated as "what we see") is no different from emptiness.
>
> Emptiness is no different from what we see.
>
> What we see is emptiness.
>
> Emptiness is found in whatever we see.
>
> This (notion of emptiness) also applies to
>
> Whatever is coming to us,
>
> Whatever we think about,
>
> Whatever we do, and
>
> Whatever we come to appreciate.

These few lines could be better understood if we make reference to another passage from the Diamond Sutra where it says:[3] "Whatever events and dharma we come across are comparable to dreams and shadows. They are as fleeting and illusory as the morning dew and lightning." The Diamond Sutra then goes on to advise us that this is the way we should evaluate the events (dharma) we see.

You will recall that toward the end of Chapter 2, I drew a distinction between the enlightened person and the common perplexed individual. The enlightened person will fully appreciate the state of emptiness, but the common perplexed individual will not. The Buddhist teaching dealing with the truth, which is beyond the apprehension of the common perplexed individual, is referred to as the true revelation.[4] For the benefit of the common perplexed individuals, certain teachings which are easily understood have been specially designed for them. They are referred to as the revelation for the common people.[5] I will explain the reason for the difference toward the end of this chapter.

When we understand the essence of what is taught in the sutras like the Diamond Sutra and the Heart Sutra, we soon appreciate that they have a common purpose in their teachings. What we find in one sutra often explains what is said in another one.

---

2   色不异空，空不异色，色即是空，空即是色，受想行识，亦复如是.
3   一切有为法，如梦幻泡影，如露亦如电，应作如是观.
4   This is referred to as "true vision" of things, 真谛.
5   This is referred to as "worldly vision" of things, 俗谛.

In very simple terms, the Diamond Sutra teaches us to have a Bodhi Resolve to do good and that when we do good, we should be unattached, unmoved, and not influenced by what we see or feel.[6] What we see is emptiness. This line of thinking may help us to understand the straightforward meaning of emptiness in Buddhist principles.

Emptiness, along with the concept of *Yuán Qǐ Fǎ* explaining how things come to happen (described in Chapter 10), is an important characteristic of Buddhism.[7] The Theravada tradition has placed a very heavy emphasis on emptiness. It is described as *sunnata*, and it is looked upon as a virtue by itself.

A very famous Thai monk by the name of Buddhadasa Bhikkhu (1906–1993) has stated in his book[8] on emptiness (therein referred to as voidness):

> To feel that there is nothing which is "me,"
>
> Without worry or doubt that anything might be "me";
>
> To feel that there is nothing which is "mine,"
>
> Without worry or doubt that anything might be "mine."

"At the moment that someone's mind is freed from these four things," Buddhadasa Bhikkhu said, "there exists what the Buddha has maintained—voidness."

When we correlate "emptiness" (or voidness) with whatever we see, you might ask if we are not adopting a policy of escapism. We are not. The following explains our position:

You will recall that toward the end of Chapter 2, I drew a distinction between the enlightened person and the common perplexed individual. The enlightened person will fully appreciate the reality of things, including the state of emptiness, but the common perplexed individual (CPI) will not. That aspect of Buddhist teachings dealing with the truth which is beyond the comprehension of the CPIs is referred to as the "true revelation."[9] For the benefit of the CPIs, certain teachings which are easily understood have been specially designed for them. They are referred to as the "revelation for the common people."[10]

---

6   应无所住而生其心 i.e., 清净心.

7   缘起性空.

8   Bhikkhu, Santikaro. 2004. *Heartwood of the Bodhi Tree: The Buddha's Teaching on Voidness*. Bangkok: Silkworm Books, p. 53–54.

9   As noted above, this is also referred to as "true vision" of things, 真谛.

10 As noted above, this is also referred to as "worldly vision" of things, 俗谛.

So, if you feel that what you see is real and find it extremely attractive, you are not alone. You are just one of the many who are not yet enlightened. Since you fail to see the situation as unreal and illusory, you have to do what you can to make the best out of it on the basis of what you see. In other words, you are supposed to follow certain rules expected to be observed by a perplexed person. You are advised to distance yourself from greed, hatred, and delusion, but you are never advised to give up your vigilance toward a meaningful life. If you have taken on a job, you should do it to the best of your ability. If you are running a business, you should try hard to make it a success. It is never the intention of Buddhists to condemn the rich and the famous just because they are rich and famous. The population of this world is necessarily made up of many different categories of people including the rich as well as the poor, the superstars and the common people. According to Buddhist principles, apart from greed, hatred, and delusion, which we must abandon, there is nothing to be criticized of a person wanting to be rich and famous, especially if that person wants to possess those qualities in order to set an example of how a person ought to behave in such a position.

I cannot end my discussion on emptiness without mentioning my experience in exchanging views on Buddhist principles with some Japanese practitioners. I recall consulting an academic for his views on the main theme of Buddhism. His reply was "Emptiness." I cannot say that he was wrong. Indeed, he was right because emptiness is a reflection of "self-nature," but if I were asked the same question, I would prefer to choose "enlightenment" or "the restoration of our self-nature" to describe the main theme. The concept that there are 84,000 ways to explain Buddhist teachings has taught us to expect different emphasis on the same principles by different people. We must try to avoid suggesting that we are right and the others are wrong.

> **An Easy Way to Understanding the Complexity of Buddhism:**
> 1. It is assumed that you know the main theme of Buddhism, and you know what it means to be enlightened.
> 2. Distinguish between "those who are enlightened"[11] and those who are not, referred to as "the common perplexed individuals."[12]

---

11 觉者.
12 凡夫.

3. Remember that the enlightened ones will know that all things are unreal and illusory. This knowledge which explains the true vision of things[13] is not easily appreciated by the common perplexed individuals. They think that everything is real.

4. For the benefit of these individuals, and knowing that they do not appreciate the truth, Buddhist teachings have devised something special for them. Ordinary people (i.e., common perplexed individuals) are taught to avoid greed, hatred, and delusion and to be mindful of the relationship of cause and consequence. This approach is what they can follow, and it is known as adopting a worldly vision of things.[14]

5. After learning Buddhism for some time, some of them may understand; the majority of them will likely remain perplexed. They will likely continue to seek worldly achievements.

6. These achievements include wealth, health, fame, recognition, and longevity. Buddhists say that there is nothing wrong with seeking these achievements. Such conduct is permissible if, and only if, the rejection of greed, hatred, and delusion is not compromised.

7. These observations will help to clarify misunderstanding in the minds of a lot of people.

---

13 俗谛.
14 真谛.

17

The Three Markings[1]

The Three Markings of Buddhism, sometimes referred to as the Three Seals of Dharma, or the Three Marks of Existence, present some very important teachings of the religion. They are referred to in certain commentaries on Buddhist teachings.[2] Specifically, they teach us that:

(1) There is no permanence or consistency in the way things come about (*zhū xíng wú cháng*).[3]
(2) We ourselves are not part of dharma (*zhū fǎ wú wǒ*),[4] and
(3) The qualities of permanence, bliss, true self, and purity are only found in the level beyond life and death called "nirvana" (*niè pán jì jìng*).[5]

There is no permanence or consistency in the way things come about.
This marking teaches us that we must recognize the fact that nothing is permanent. No event or situation is a norm. We must not take things for granted. The good fortune of a person may suddenly disappear due to some unpredictable causes. It is said, by way of illustration, "the sea might turn into arable land, and sentient beings become dust." Things are changing by the split second. What happened a moment ago is history, and the future will never be the same as we find it at this moment in time.

Some readers might ask: I know the sun is going to rise tomorrow morning. How can we say that there is no norm? How would you explain this day-and-night phenomenon which will likely continue on indefinitely? The answer is: First, Buddhism believes that there is a perfect system. The system was brought about by self-nature. Both self-nature and the system it brought about are perfect.

---

1 三法印.
2 大智度论二十二.
3 诸行无常.
4 诸法无我.
5 涅盘寂静.

The system works in eternity. The system provides for many, many rules and regulations; some of which we know, such as the law of motion, the law of gravity, the general theory of relativity, etc. It also provides for the operation of *Yuán Qǐ Fǎ* as described in Chapter 10 to govern how things come about. Now, coming back to the day-and-night scenario, the earth rotates around the sun. This must be the result of certain causes and consequences. Buddhists call them the initiating cause and the sustaining cause. If the sustaining cause disappears, the existing scenario will come to an end. Nobody would like to predict what impact the disaster would have on us as beings living on this planet. Until the sustaining cause disappears, things will remain as they are.

We ourselves are not part of dharma.
We are taught not to be self-centered. If we truly appreciate that we are not part of dharma, we will be less inclined to put our own personal interests ahead of the interests of others. According to Buddhist principles, neither we ourselves nor any events we come across possess any quality of permanence like our self-nature. The Diamond Sutra says specifically that all dharma, including ourselves, is illusory and unreal. Possibly because Buddhism claims that our existence is illusory and unreal, some writers say that "Buddhism stands unique in the history of human thought in denying the existence of a soul."[6] This line of argument rocks the foundation of Buddhism. It suggests that the termination of life is comparable to putting out a burning candle, so that upon the demise of a person, everything will come to an abrupt end. All our deeds will be washed away without any consequences. This is certainly contrary to our basic understanding of Buddhism.

It is true that the term *soul*, as understood in Christianity, is not used in Buddhism. However, the belief in the inevitable relationship between cause and consequence is testimony that upon a person's demise, some spiritual "state" or "medium" must exist to receive the reward or punishment. This "state" or "medium" is not referred to as a soul. It is known by a different name.[7]

Is there a "self" in Buddhism? When we say that we are not part of dharma, we already accept that there is no self. Yet, according to the Diamond Sutra in Article 25, the ordinary, uninformed person[8] thinks that there is a self. These people think that all dharma and events including ourselves are real. The enlightened ones think that all these are illusory and unreal. Looking at things from the angle of the Buddha, there cannot be a distinction between the "enlightened" and "the

---

6   Rahula, Walpola. 2005. *What The Buddha Taught*. Finland: Oneworld Publications, p. 51.
7   The Chinese would refer to the spiritual state as 神识 or 阿赖耶识.
8   Referred to as 凡夫.

ordinary, perplexed individuals." The difference arises out of human aspirations. In other words, the issue of whether there is a self arises out of human aspirations. We should learn to look at things from the angle of the Buddha and ignore the difference.

The qualities of permanence, bliss, true self, and purity are only found beyond life and death in the level called "nirvana."
This defines the state of nirvana as possessing the qualities of permanence, bliss, true self, and purity. A person who becomes enlightened is said to enter nirvana when his bodily life comes to an end. In this state, suffering will come to an end. We are taught to appreciate the desirability of the qualities of nirvana. The Nirvana Sutra has explained in some detail the eight tastes of nirvana.[9] Perhaps we could imagine nirvana as the bliss of life in heaven.

It is interesting that the same concepts of Buddhism are often repeated in different contexts. For example, as we have discussed, the Bodhisattva's Big Eight Appreciations Sutra has conveyed a message similar to what is essentially taught in the Three Markings.

In the First Appreciation in Bodhisattva's Big Eight Appreciations Sutra,, it is stated that:
1. Nothing is permanent in this world.
2. The security of our land is brittle.
3. Matters are sadly void in essence.
4. The five elements we encounter are not part of us.
5. The very existence of things comes and goes.
6. It is deceptive and devoid of a central theme.
7. The mind is the source of all evils.
8. The appearance provides evidence of sin.
9. If we can look at things from this perspective,
10. Gradually, we shall feel detached from life and death.

---

9   1. 常住 三际常存十方恒在。; 2. 寂灭 寂绝无为大患永灭。; 3. 不老 不迁不变无增无灭。; 4. 不死 从本不生今亦无灭。; 5. 清净 安住清净诸障悉尽。; 6. 虚通 虚彻灵通圆融无碍。; 7. 不动 寂然不动妙绝无为。; 8. 快乐 无生死苦有真常乐.

Line 1 refers to the impermanence of things. This is a reflection of the first marking.

Line 4 refers to us being part of the impermanence. It refers to the need to adopt a selfless attitude. Self-nature as our true self does not form part of the dharma, and it is permanent in nature. Our body as well as everything around us is not permanent. This reflects what is taught in the second marking.

Line 10 refers to nirvana as a detachment from life and death. It reflects what is taught in the third marking.

The Three Markings are core concepts of Buddhism. Every serious student should know about them. They convey a message that is philosophical in nature rather than a religious one. For an average person to try to understand what Buddhism is about, it is essential that he/she should first understand the basic features described in Chapter 2 and then understand the other theories including the Three Markings as a spice to appreciate the basic core values of Buddhism.

18

The One Unity Perception[1]

We shall now discuss a Buddhist concept that has the greatest potential to promote global peace and harmony, the *One Unity Perception*.

We have already seen how the three poisons—namely, greed, hatred, and delusion—blocked our self-nature and how their removal would restore it. We say that these three elements are the major cause of conflicts. This argument is simple, and yet it is convincing. In fact, we could also advance another argument to substantiate why Buddhism could solve conflicts.

This is the principle that "what comprises the universe and everything in it should be treated as one."

There is now scientific proof that the universe originated from what is called "the big bang." The big bang started with what is known as a "singularity." Through measuring the distance between planets today as compared with what it was in the past, scientists have ascertained that the whole universe has been expanding and is still expanding. Based on scientific data, they can also give a fair estimate of the beginning of the universe, starting from singularity.

The Tan Sutra states that self-nature was capable of the creation of everything, naturally including the big bang. My deduction is that self-nature brought about a perfect system. Through this system, including the application of *Yuán Qǐ Fǎ*, the big bang came about. Thus, when the big bang exploded starting from singularity, there must have been an initiating cause and a triggering cause. If the universe started from singularity, at least, the entire universe was one at that moment in time.

How does one unit in the universe respond when it sees that another unit therein is hurt? Consider the following illustration: If the sole of my foot treads on a needle, seeing that something has gone wrong, the other parts of my body would readily come to the rescue. In this case, they would lend a helping hand to remove the needle. This is the consequence of "oneness." The help is spontaneous. No reason is needed. If, for some reason, my teeth accidentally bite my tongue, surely my tongue would not think of revenge or doing anything to punish my

---

1　一合相 in Section 30 of the Diamond Sutra.

teeth. Buddhist principles teach us that when we are hurt, we do not seek revenge, like our tongue would not seek revenge against the teeth that have bitten it. This is another illustration to explain the effect of "oneness." When we truly appreciate that our opponents and ourselves are one, we are much more inclined to forgive them rather than to seek to impose punishment. The policy of an eye for an eye is contrary to Buddhist principles. If more people would adopt this attitude of oneness, the world would undoubtedly be a safer place to live in. This is the value of Buddhism in the promotion of peace and harmony.

The One Unity Perception is also useful to explain why we extend filial piety to our parents and why we respect our ancestors. Not only do we look upon ourselves and our contemporaries as one, we also include people living before us and those living after us as one. This approach has provided us with a good reason to respect our ancestors.

Where in the sutras could we find reference to the "One Unity Perception"? Article 30 of the Diamond Sutra is directly on the point. It says that if the universe *were* real, then there would be "one unity perception." Buddhist principles teach us that the universe and all dharma we encounter are unreal and illusory. How then could we talk of a "One Unity Perception"? According to the same Article 30, those who are enlightened will not talk about this perception. Those who are not yet enlightened will think that whatever they encounter is real. Presumably, the One Unity Perception is mentioned for the benefit of those not yet enlightened.

Today, we know how important it is to try to do what we can to preserve and not to damage the environment. Two thousand five hundred years ago, Buddhism had already provided us with a good reason to love the environment.

The need to respect life is an important requirement in both Christianity and Buddhism. The Fifth Commandment says: "Thou shall not kill." We are taught not to kill other human beings. The Ten Commandments never suggest that we should not kill other species of life. We are not sure whether from the point of view of Christians, we should treat the other beings as a source of food for human consumption. The first of the "Three Blessings of Tranquility (Blessing of Heaven and Man)"[2] requires us to be compassionate and forbids the killing other sentient beings. Read with the theory of oneness, we know we don't kill because they are part of us.

Now that we understand the various blessings stated in Chapter 6 and the One Unity Perception, we should understand the logic of a very famous saying in Buddhism,[3] which could be translated as:

---

2 See Chapter 6 above.
3 无缘大慈，同体大悲.

1. The Great Compassion is rational love without a cause; and
2. Being in the same unity is the root of such compassion.

The first line refers to the frame of mind a Bodhisattva has when he thinks of giving away something to someone. He does not have a reason to give this something away other than the hope that the receiver will benefit from it. The message to convey is that Bodhi Resolve does not require a cause for us to show compassion. This is worth mentioning because it looks as though it is an exception to the general concept of *Yuán Qǐ Fǎ* as explained in Chapter 10, which says that everything has a cause. The rationale is that when we extend compassion to others, compassion is grounds by itself; there is no other cause for our conduct.

The second line refers to the idea that because all is one, our perceived enemies and we are one. They are like different parts of a body. The lesson to learn is: We should not do anything to hurt the other parts of our own body. We should not even perceive them as our enemy.

Some Buddhist teachers like to say that Buddhism is all about suffering and its removal. I think there is a need to clarify this statement for the benefit of beginners. This is my logic: Buddhism is about enlightenment. Through enlightenment, we will know how to remove our suffering. Buddhism is not about the direct removal of suffering. It is not a painkiller or a pill that numbs our senses.

The One Unity Perception

A Simple Guide to Appreciating the Big Picture of Buddhism

1. I do not pretend that Buddhism is easy to understand. In learning Buddhism, we are learning the truth about life and the environment surrounding life, including the universe. We must know that Buddhism has the main theme and ultimate goal of showing us how to get enlightened. Through enlightenment, we obtain happiness.

2. To understand the big picture of Buddhism, we must learn its core principles and values. These are found in Chapter 2. Buddhism has also provided us with some rather comprehensive guidelines and logic for the steps we take in our daily lives. A specimen of such guidelines is found in Chapter 6.

3. In the course of our analysis of Buddhist principles, we may come across concepts not covered by this book. We must try to understand how these concepts fit into the big picture. We must know how to find a place to store these new concepts without having them clash with the main theme.

Part 3

Reasons for Skepticism and Suspicion about Buddhism

What are the more important problems people face in promoting Buddhism? To convince someone to take up Christianity is a relatively simple affair. The following dialogue explains why and how the author was introduced to the Roman Catholic faith over sixty years ago. A priest in the primary school attended by the author posed the following questions. The author, who supplied the answers, was then a boy of seven:

Q: Look at the sculpture out there. Do you agree that someone must have created it before it could exist?
A: Yes, someone must have built it.

Q: So even for Planet Earth and everything that is in it, do you agree there must be a creator?
A: Yes, I agree.

Q: That creator is God. So do you agree there is a God who created the earth and everything in it?
A: I do.

Q: So do you believe in God, and do you obey his command?
A: I do.

Through this short session of question and answer, we see that the Catholic Church has already succeeded in recruiting a young follower to the Christian faith. Buddhism is relatively difficult to understand, especially for young children. The logic of Buddhism is for the relatively mature mind. As one writer puts it, "Buddhism is not anti-intellectual. It has a profound and elaborate philosophical dimension."[1] To understand Buddhism, we must segregate the essentials from the inessentials. In doing so, it is not difficult to obtain a breakthrough in appreciating what Buddhism teaches. Understanding is still some way from enlightenment.

There is no shortage of scholars who place emphasis on the relatively less important aspects of Buddhism and treat them as the focus. This creates a wrong impression of Buddhism. There is also no shortage of authors repeating these misconceptions. How do we distinguish what is the main focus and what is not? Buddhism teaches us that we should not insist upon "us" being right and others, "them," being wrong. We should consult what is stated in the sutras for guidance. There are said to be eighty-four thousand ways to promote the right ideas. But if we place emphasis on something that is not the most important, we miss the true concept of Buddhism. The less important ideas will continue to dominate.

Earlier on, I compared the logic of Buddhism with the logic of Christianity. I will now deal with some of the misconceptions about Buddhism and hope that they can be dispelled:

a. The misunderstanding about Theravada and Mahayana. This aspect will be discussed in the following chapter.

b. The misunderstanding about the relationship between the various "schools of thought" in promoting Buddhism. This aspect will be discussed in Chapter 20.

c. The explanation of certain concepts, e.g., "emptiness," "the Four Noble Truths," "the Eight Rightful Paths," in isolation and without reference to the ultimate goal in Buddhism. These concepts are admittedly important. Yet, placing too heavy an emphasis on them will not help us to understand the big picture. This aspect will be discussed in Chapter 21.

d. The misconception that Buddhism is polytheistic. This aspect will be discussed in Chapter 22.

---

1   Morris, Tony. 2006. *What Do Buddhists Believe?* London: Granta Books, p. 1.

19

Explanation of the Theravada[1] and Mahayana[2] Perspectives

When Buddha Shakyamuni introduced the Buddhist faith, he preached "enlightenment." The main theme of Buddhism was never in doubt.

According to what is stated in the Buddha Conservation Sutra,[3] the basic distinction between Theravada and Mahayana was nothing more than a reference to different stages of cultivation. In this sutra, the Buddha discussed the different stages of cultivation at some length. Theravada Buddhism is established on the human-heavenly basis, which includes filial respect, respectfulness to our teachers and elders, compassion to others, and diligence in practicing the Ten Virtuous Conducts. This is the foundation.[4] With this as a base, we can meet the criteria to begin learning and practicing Buddhism. The Buddha is reported to have said in this sutra that all Buddhist students should have completed learning what is taught at the Theravada level before proceeding to learn the teachings at the Mahayana level.[5]

Yet, this was only a point of view expressed in the Buddha Conservation Sutra. The reality is that Buddhist practitioners in many countries in Southeast Asia today follow the Theravada tradition. These countries include Sri Lanka, Myanmar, Thailand, and Laos, and they receive the support of their governments.

Why was there a split between Theravada and Mahayana, and why were different schools established within the Mahayana environment? After the death of Shakyamuni, his followers continued to explain Buddhism generation after generation. Along the way, emphasis began to be placed in different areas. This is not surprising, as we are advised that there are eighty-four thousand ways to learn

---

1   小乘佛法. The term *Theravada* is loosely used in this book to include Hinayana or Hinayanan Buddhism.
2   大乘佛法.
3   佛藏经.
4   See Chapter 6 above.
5   The exact words as translated were "不先学小乘，后学大乘，非佛弟子."

Buddhism. In the Diamond Sutra, the Buddha has said that whatever we encounter may be the Buddha's Dharma. No wonder different schools are set up. Yet, in spite of the establishment of different schools, the basic features of Buddhism have remained the same. If someone tries to promote some religious ideas where the basic features of Buddhism are not upheld, we can only say that it is an attempt to introduce a new religion. As the two different perspectives developed, one group (Theravada Buddhists, or Buddhists with a Theravada perspective) thought that the most important object of life was to enlighten oneself and achieve nirvana. One was free to help others and to work toward this noble destination, but self-elevation was the most important mission. The Agama Sutra says effectively that upon the removal of suffering when one enters nirvana:

> My life has come to an end.
>
> My work in inspiring spiritual values is established.
>
> What I set out to do is done.
>
> I have no reason to face rebirths.[6]

Another group (Mahayana Buddhists, or Buddhists with a Mahayana perspective) felt that one should build up and extend a selfless desire to help others.[7] Their beliefs are expressed in the Four Grand Wishes:[8]

1. There is no limit to the number of sentient beings around, and I vow to help them cultivate.
2. There is no end to the feeling of annoyance, and I vow to get rid of it.
3. There is no limit to the vastness of Buddhist teachings, and I vow to learn them.
4. There is no goal higher than Buddhahood, and I vow to reach that destination.

The goal of Mahayana Buddhism, therefore, is perfection. One would not feel comfortable until all are saved. This is the heart of Bodhisattva.

How would a Buddhist follower, in particular a Mahayana Buddhist, interpret the split? We must always remember the undisputable fact that there are different

---

6   我生已盡，梵行已立，所作已辦，不受後有。
7   发菩提心.
8   四宏愿：众生无边誓愿度，烦恼无尽誓愿断，法门无量誓愿学，佛道无上誓愿成。.

ways to reach enlightenment. It is not consistent with Buddhist teachings for us to claim that we are right and the others are wrong.

One point of concern is that if we do not extend our help to others when we can, we won't feel comfortable. We don't feel comfortable because there is some room for improvement before we can reach perfection. To be perfect, one must have the Bodhi Resolve.

How would a Theravada follower interpret the split? In the words of Huston Smith, a well-known academic in religious studies: "If one were to transcend self-centeredness completely as the Arhat do, what would be left but compassion?"[9] The answer is "Nothing." Yet, this answer prompts another question: If one were so full of compassion, how could one feel comfortable when one enters into the Western World of Supreme Happiness leaving others behind facing the risk of rebirth? After a full circle, the Four Grand Wishes and the Bodhi Resolve are the only solution.

Could we simply have studied Mahayana and ignored Theravada practices? Definitely not. The reason is this: We would have missed the basics of Buddhism. We must not start to learn the more advanced teachings without a solid foundation. We would have done exactly what the Buddha in the Buddha Conservation Sutra advised us not to do.

The advancement of the Theravada tradition is not detrimental to the Mahayana tradition. The reverse is also true. Indeed, one is beneficial to the other because their teachings supplement each other.

Many scholars of the Theravada tradition think that the Four Noble Truths have covered the essence of Buddhism or inferred what it is. For the reasons I shall set out in the following paragraph, I agree they have a point. Yet, I still think that for a novice student coming into contact with Buddhist teachings for the first time, he/she would understand Buddhism better if the teacher tells him/her that the essence is in the two features as mentioned in Chapter 2.

I agree that the Four Noble Truths have implicitly referred to all aspects of the two basic features of Buddhism for the following reasons:

The Third Noble Truth refers to "nirvana" to be attained when suffering is removed. The use of the term "nirvana" implies knowledge of (a) the six realms, (b) the possibility of one avoiding the rebirth cycle, and (c) the ability to restore one's self-nature. The restoration of self-nature is the essence of the first of the two features.

---

9   Smith, Huston. 1991. *The World's Religions: Our Great Wisdom Traditions.* New York: Harper Collins, p. 127.

The six realms and the rebirth cycle are used to make sure that good deeds will be rewarded and bad deeds punished. This is the essence of the second of the two features.

It is therefore clear that the Four Noble Truths have effectively referred to the two main features of Buddhism. For this reason, I can say that in so far as the main features of Buddhism are concerned, both the Theravada tradition and the Mahayana tradition have a similar focus, viz., the desirability of avoiding the six realms.

This explanation is very important, because only when both Theravada and Mahayana share the same focus can we safely say that we have Buddhism in two branches and not two religions having some of their teachings in common.

Why are we so keen to explain the difference in the perspectives? The governments of some of the countries in Southeast Asia where Buddhism is practiced support the Theravada tradition. The people there are already confused because of the difference, which they don't quite understand. If we fail to do anything to put the record straight, the direction given by the Buddha Conservation Sutra will not be known. We are not putting up a new argument in the twenty-first century. We are only following the advice given to us two thousand years ago. There is already talk of setting up a "new vehicle" to be called "Navayana" for the Western world. If this should happen, and if the principles of Buddhism were thereby misinterpreted, people would get even more confused, and the uninformed public in the Western world would be the ones who would suffer most.

Perfection of Buddhism in the Mahayana Perspective

The following question-and-answer session represents the first lesson in Catholicism the author learned as a primary student:

Q: Why are we in this world?
A: We are in this world to worship God and to save our souls.

So, the aim of life in Christianity is to save our souls. It is rather similar to the Theravada perspective of Buddhism where the aim is enlightenment and achieving nirvana for ourselves. The Mahayana perspective is somewhat different. Mahayana tradition talks of perfection and of the Bodhi Resolve. The Bodhisattva of Mahayana has the goal of helping all sentient beings to get enlightened.

20

Understanding the Rise of Schools of Thought in Buddhism

Different schools of thought were established usually when some prominent leaders of Buddhism, mostly very learned, thought that they had discovered a better way to interpret Buddhist teachings. A new methodology was usually introduced at the same time to help the followers to reach enlightenment. Later in this chapter, we will explain how one of these schools—to be specific, the first of such schools—came to be established.

Why were there different schools of thought? We could advance a few reasons, but we would merely be speculating. You may have your own ideas, which you may want to add to the following list. There were different schools of thought because:

1. It is against Buddhist principles to insist upon someone being right and others being wrong. This attitude results in liberalization in the way Buddhist principles are interpreted. This free-for-all attitude is conducive to the acceptance of different interpretations of Buddhist philosophy. The good thing is that it also results in serious clashes being avoided.
2. There has never been any central governing body to control the ideology of Buddhism. Again, it is also against Buddhist principles to claim superiority of one ideology over and above the others.
3. There is no central governing body to supervise religious activities and practices.
4. A charismatic religious leader would want to create an identity. The best way to do so was to establish a school of thought. For practical purposes, there were also other reasons to establish a new school. For example, a new school was quite convenient to be used as a means to preserve one's uniqueness and to foster a better relationship with the authorities.
5. In Chapter 6, we mentioned that there are Three Gems of Buddhism. They are: the Buddha, the precepts, and the monks. In fact, it is the

value of the quality behind these three items that Buddhists treasure. A particular school might have its own way to look at such values. Besides, different schools might take the point that knowledge or enlightenment could be better acquired through different approaches.

This is not unlike people learning Chinese kung fu, a term used to refer to martial arts for self-defense. Students may want to learn tài jí quán, tái quán dào, yǒng chūn quán, jiujitsu, or a host of other techniques. The ultimate objective of learning martial arts is to learn how to protect oneself in a fight. The goal of following the teachings of a particular school in Buddhism is to learn how to reach enlightenment. In both cases, they have a common objective, but each school uses a different means.

In Buddhist study, it is possible to classify the different schools of thought into three categories:

1. A school where students are taught of sudden appreciation, that is, where one would likely achieve a breakthrough in learning Buddhism all of a sudden and not as a result of following a course with gradual progress. (A breakthrough and enlightenment are not identical in that a person may obtain a breakthrough in understanding the principles and yet may not be able to practice giving up worldly attachments and could not therefore achieve enlightenment.)
2. A school where the precepts, as well as the sutras, will be taught one by one, and the students acquire gradual progress in their correct understanding of Buddhism through gradual appreciation and eventually get a breakthrough.
3. A school where purity and tranquility are stressed as the two basic elements in our cultivation leading us toward the route to a breakthrough.

When we start to learn the principles of Buddhism, we can enter any one of the schools. After we have learned what is taught, we will realize that it would have made little difference which school we joined since all the schools had the same objective of leading students toward the restoration of their self-nature.

There are presently seven better-known schools of thought in Buddhism. They include one school of sudden appreciation (*chan zong*[1]), four schools of gradual

---

1 禅宗.

Understanding the Rise of Schools of Thought in Buddhism   103

appreciation (*tiān tái zōng*,[2] *huā yán zōng*,[3] *sān lùn zōng*,[4] and *fǎ huá zōng*[5]), and two schools of purity (*jìng tǔ zōng*[6] and *mì zōng*[7]). In spite of the existence of these different schools of thought, it is always important to remember that the main theme of Buddhism remains the same in all the schools.

The First School of Thought—Tian Tai School (Tiān tái zōng)
We will now explain how a typical school would come into being. Let us imagine ourselves living in China about fourteen hundred years ago. An absolute monarch rules the country. Anyone desiring to promote a religion cannot start without the blessing of the highest authority, namely the monarchy. If we had the blessing of the highest authority, because of human weakness, we would probably want to keep it away from the other practitioners. The best way to preserve that blessing was to build an identity and to foster a good relationship with the people in power. It would be ideal if we had some specialty in the way we interpreted the Buddhist philosophy.

The founder of *tiān tái zōng* did exactly as described above when the first school of thought was formed in China.
During the reign of King Zhōu Wǔ-dì[8] (560–578), the Buddhist practitioners had become extremely immoral and corrupt. King Zhou Wǔ-dì decided that he could not tolerate the situation any longer and ordered all monasteries to be closed and all the properties of those monasteries to be confiscated. After the death of King Zhōu Wǔ-dì, a renowned scholar named Zhìyǐ[9] (538–597) seized the opportunity to reestablish Buddhism. With a new theory,[10] he developed a new identity for Buddhist teachings. He promoted the idea that the truth of things would depend on the needs of reality.[11] Of course, the theory was much more complicated and

---

2   天台宗.
3   华严宗.
4   三论宗.
5   法华宗.
6   净土宗.
7   密宗.
8   周武帝.
9   智顗.
10 即事而真, the idea was that the truth of any theory must be capable of being applied to the facts at the time. This philosophy is strikingly similar to the philosophy of the government of modern China which says that "the only way to ascertain the truth is through pragmatic experience" 实践是检验真理的唯一标准.
11 Zeng, Qi-hai. 2006. *Discussion on the Three Schools of Thought*. Shanghai: Shanghai Chinese Academy of Social Sciences Publishing House, p. 17–18. (See http://www.

profound than this simple statement. On the promotion of Buddhist teaching, Zhìyī introduced new rules and pragmatic applications of what he taught.[12]

The founder of *tiān tái zōng* befriended the highest authorities with his new concept, and he firmly established the first school of thought for Buddhism in China.

The Esoteric School of Thought (Mì zōng)
The Esoteric School came into being through the effort of three very learned monks known as Shànwúwèi (637–735), Jīngāngzhì (669–741), and Bùkòng (705–774).[13] They introduced a new concept, but the main theme of Buddhism remained the same.[14] The first monastery for the Esoteric School is said to be the Dà Xīng Shàn Sì[15] in Shǎnxī Province. Different schools often use different sutras as their basic reference materials. The sutra principally used for the Esoteric School is the Big Sun Sutra.[16]

Some writers like to refer to the Esoteric School as the Vajrayana tradition. It is interesting to note that in the Esoteric School, there are distinctions between the Red Sect, the Yellow Sect, the White Sect, the Katya Sect, and the Black Sect. Yet the basic central theme of Buddhism is kept by all. For example, in a ritual known as "The Golden Cicada Sheds Its Shell"[17] practiced by the Black Sect Tantric Buddhists, the restoration of one's "true self" (or self-nature)[18] is clearly referred to.

His Holiness, the Dalai Lama, is a leader of a Yellow Sect of the Esoteric School of Thought. The Yellow Sect has the largest followings.

The Hua Yan School of Thought (Huā yán zōng)
The Hua Yan School of Thought was famous for the contribution it made in the development of Buddhist philosophy and the Mahayana traditions in China. This school uses the Flower Adornment Sutra as its main reference and guidance for its theory. The core theology of the Hua Yan School of Thought is traditionally sum-

---

sassp.com).
12 Ibid., 77–78.
13 善无畏，金刚智，and 不空.
14 Lin, Yan-jiao. 2000. *A Tour of Chinese Buddhism*. Hebei: Hebei Education Publishers, p. 99–107.
15 大兴善寺.
16 大日经.
17 金蝉脱壳.
18 还我本真.

marized in two points[19] namely (1) that purity of mind as reflected in Buddha's nature is responsible for the origin of all events and (2) that there is perfection and compatibility in Buddhist philosophy as explained in the various schools.

Point (1) carries a meaning similar to or consistent with the revelation in the Tan Sutra where it says that self-nature (which is the nature of Buddha) is capable of originating and did originate all dharma and the universe.

One argument advanced by the Hua Yan School, which many novice students find difficult to understand, is that "one is all and all is one."[20] This argument could be interpreted as follows: Before reaching enlightenment, probably everybody will find the various phenomena they come across to be serious and important. They include[21] birth, growing old, failure in one's health, and finally death. Also important are fame, wealth, recognition, and condemnation. Buddhism maintains that this line of thinking is contrary to what the Buddha teaches us. For example, the Diamond Sutra is quite unequivocal when it says that all events (dharma) are illusory and unreal. Being unreal, there cannot be any distinction between one of such events as mentioned above and the rest of them. On this account, the Hua Yan School promotes the idea that one is all, and all is one.

The Pure Land School of Thought (Jìng tǔ zōng)

The specialty of the Pure Land School, a very popular school and the one to which Master Chin Kung belongs, may be summarized as follows:

1. It uses what is known as Five Pure Land Sutras and One Treatise as its chief sutra and reference to teach its followers.
2. The development of purity in the mind is an important goal. It places emphasis on the desirability of chanting the name of the Buddha for cultivation.
3. Its followers believe in the need to find their way to the Western World of Supreme Happiness.
4. It recommends a mode of cultivation through a belief, a willingness, and an action taken.[22] The belief is that a student must have confidence in

---

19 「法界缘起」 and 「圆融无碍」. 法界 = 「一真法界」 = 「一心法界」 = 「如来藏自性清净心」 = 自性. 「圆融无碍」 = 「圆满无缺，融汇一切」.
20 一即一切，一切即一.
21 生老病死，生离死别，名成利就，名闻利养.
22 信愿行.

himself or herself, confidence about help from the Buddha, and confidence in his or her ability to analyze things including the relationship between cause and consequence. The willingness is a desire to go to the Western World of Supreme Happiness and then to come back to help others.[23] The action to be taken includes remembering the Buddha and chanting his name and following what is taught in the precepts, that is to say, to do good and stop doing what is bad.[24]

One should not be surprised if at some point of time in the future, other schools of thought are established. This is perfectly in order provided the basic theme of Buddhism remains intact.

You might want to ask which school you should join. There is no definite answer. The type of training you think could help you get a breakthrough in your understanding of Buddhism should determine which school will suit you best.

Perhaps an elementary student in Buddhism does not have to concern himself or herself with the specific theory of each school of thought. It is probably sufficient to have a general idea of what the schools are, why they were established, and how they are different.

Suppose a person, having started to study Buddhism based upon the interpretation of a particular school, finds out that there is some ideology or practice within that school that he or she cannot accept. Does he or she have a duty to compromise his or her own feelings and follow the crowd? Or does he or she have the right to differ? It is submitted that Buddhism has sufficient capacity to accept different views. One should be free to make one's own choice. I make this observation because I have in mind a practice which, for obvious reasons, many of us will not be able to accept—of "tantric union of polarities when dissolving selfhood, a couple could enjoy attentive, mutually appreciative, enlightened contemplation."[25]

When you understand the basic concept of Buddhism, you will appreciate that the schools must respect each other. The first lesson Buddhism has taught us is that Buddhists need to avoid the insistence of one's perception or one's rights being upheld at the expense of others or for one's benefit. Each of the schools has its own way to teach Buddhism. It is not for anyone to allege that one particular way is correct and the others are wrong. Yet, you must have the right to differ when you feel that things are not what they should be.

---

23 专修往生，乖愿再来。
24 持佛名号，止恶修善。
25 Gach, Gary. 2004. *The Complete Idiot's Guide to Understanding Buddhism (2nd ed)*. New York: Alpha Books, p. 250. This practice is referred to as 男女双修。

21

The Problem of Missing the Main Theme of Buddhism

In Chapter 2, we explained the two most essential features of Buddhism as (1) the ability to understand about ourselves and everything around us through removing perplexity and doubt and (2) appreciating the inevitable relationship between cause and consequence. We do not intend to spend time explaining the same principles here.

In a place like Hong Kong, where the inhabitants are predominantly ethnically Chinese, people are perfectly free to follow the religion of their choice, and many like to call themselves Buddhists. They might not have participated in any ceremony like baptism in a Roman Catholic Church. When you ask them to explain what exactly Buddhism is about, most of them will honestly admit: "I don't know." Some will say, "I hope to get protection from heaven above." Many will give you an answer like, "Good deeds will bring forth good consequences." While the last mentioned answer has pointed in the right direction, it is still not a satisfactory answer. The reality is that it is not easy to give a simple answer.

What do Buddhist teachings lead us to? What is the destination? What should we do to reach that destination? Until these questions are answered, we have not yet explained what Buddhism is about. As long as the main theme is not well defined, people will continue to miss the value of Buddhist teachings. When we fail to find a focus in spite of the fact that we may be loaded with information, we will not find the teachings attractive.

If then we refer to the books available on the market to try to find out from the existing materials on Buddhism, we will very likely get confused and be disappointed. We can safely say that many of the authors who write on Buddhism want to find out the correct answers themselves.

A host of questions are at the back of the mind of the uninformed about the exciting subject of Buddhism. We have summarized the essence of the issues that deserve our attention, and we shall attempt to answer all the questions raised.

The Questions

1. What constitutes the basic principle of Buddhism? What is the most important of Buddhist teachings? What precisely does it mean to be enlightened? Is belief in rebirth essential?
2. What constitutes Theravada? What constitutes Mahayana? What is the distinction between Theravada and Mahayana?
3. Why are there different schools of thought in Buddhism? Why do they coexist with each other?
4. When the basic principle of Buddhism is not clear, should we talk about Buddhisms in the plural and focus on their practices rather than searching for a set of universal premises?
5. Some analyst has said that "Buddhists are not primarily concerned with believing and thinking; their main interests are being and doing." Is that true?
6. How much has Buddhism changed since the days of Shakyamuni?
7. What are the qualifications to be a Buddhist? What should one do to become one?
8. What do Buddhists say and do?
9. Do Buddhists apply what they learn to what they do?
10. Why is Buddhism meaningful? How does Buddhism change our way of life?

The Answers

1. What constitutes the basic principle of Buddhism? What is the most important of Buddhist teachings? What precisely does it mean to be enlightened? Is belief in rebirth essential?

   Chapter 2 has provided an answer to these basic questions. We do not share the view, as one writer puts it, that "Buddhists seem to disagree about some apparently very basic 'theological' questions."[1] It is fundamental that Buddhists believe in rebirths and in the inevitable relationship between cause and consequence. The other basic concept is self-nature. These are fundamental and basic. A person cannot claim to understand Buddhism if he or she does not see these points.

---

1   Morris, Tony. 2006. *What Do Buddhists Believe?* London: Granta Books, p. 4.

Chinese people seem to have less difficulty than Westerners finding the main theme of Buddhism. I came to this conclusion after reading a book on Taoism.[2] It is said that two aspects of Buddhism have merged into and form part of the Taoist concepts. These two aspects happen to be the two main features of Buddhism as I mentioned in Chapter 2. The importance of these two features is evident as they were faithfully followed in the two major religions in China—Buddhism and Taoism.

2. What constitutes Theravada? What constitutes Mahayana? What is the distinction between Theravada and Mahayana?

One needs to know the main focus of Buddhism before one can understand and appreciate the difference between Theravada and Mahayana (see Chapter 19). As we have explained, the Buddha Conservation Sutra was very explicit in its explanation.

3. Why are there different schools of thought in Buddhism? Why do they coexist with each other?

A basic essential quality of Buddhism is not to insist upon oneself being right and others being wrong. This liberal attitude allowed practitioners to adopt different interpretations of Buddhist philosophy. The good thing about such liberalism is the avoidance of clashes and the maintenance of peaceful coexistence amongst Buddhism's followers. The bad thing is that practitioners need to be reminded of the main focus of Buddhism from time to time. Otherwise, we may find ourselves treading along a course deviated from the original teaching of its founder.

4. When the basic principle of Buddhism is not clear, should we talk about Buddhisms in the plural and focus on their practices rather than searching for a set of universal premises?

The basic principle of Buddhism is quite clear. It has a focus. All the various schools established so far share the same focus. Any philosopher claiming to be specialized in religious studies may have some new ideas and may want to set up a new religion in the future. That is his prerogative and what he does has nothing to do with Buddhism. But if he wants to set up a new school of thought in Buddhism, then he must share the same ideology of Buddhism as the author has tried to explain in Chapter 2. Again, the basic principle of Buddhism is very clear. There is no reason to think of Buddhisms in the plural. As for the practices, each school has its own ideas. It is not in keeping

---

2 Wang, Qia. 2005. *Basic Knowledge of Taosim in China*. Beijing: Publishers for Religion and Culture, p. 6.

with the principles of Buddhism for any school to claim that it is correct and the others are wrong.

5. Some analyst has said that "Buddhists are not primarily concerned with believing and thinking; their main interests are being and doing." Is that true?

It is true that Buddhist principles are pragmatic. They are mainly based on practical application. Yet, *believing* is also a necessary ingredient. A Buddhist must believe in the concept of self-nature, which is identical to Buddha's nature, and the inevitable relationship of cause and consequence. What is remarkable is that one does not have to understand the Four Noble Truths or the Eight Rightful Paths to claim that one knows what Buddhism is about, although so many books now available in the market have placed such a heavy emphasis on them.

6. How much has Buddhism changed since the days of Shakyamuni?

The core principles of Buddhism have not changed since day one.[3] Theravada and Mahayana were already referred to in the Buddha's sutras from the very beginning.

We now know that life on Earth has been in existence for over three and a half billion years. Man has existed for no more than three and a half million years. A religious principle, if it is to be accepted as the truth, or the universal truth, should hold true at all times. The concept of rebirth in Buddhism is applicable to man and all sentient beings. It should have been in place and should not have been changed during the three and a half billion years. Indeed, based on Buddhist principles, the rebirth cycle is exactly what should have happened throughout all these years.

7. What are the qualifications to be a Buddhist? What should we do to become one?

Anyone who understands the basic principles of Buddhism (or the relevant parts of such principles) and who accepts such basic principles could be called a Buddhist. There is no prerequisite of any ceremony involved, although the formal allegiance as stated in Chapter 6 is an option. If someone changes his mind afterward, he can say that he is no longer a Buddhist follower. There are no penalties and no hard feelings. There is complete freedom. A person who does not believe in Buddhism would not be looked down upon in a Buddhist community. There is no pressure arising out of a change of identity following a change in one's faith. A person marrying into a Buddhist family has a free choice of whether or not to share and whether to stop sharing the faith of the

---

3 The moment Shakyamuni became enlightened.

other members of the family. It is not unusual for the members of the same family to have different religious faiths, and there is no problem with that from the Buddhist standpoint.

8. What do Buddhists say and do?

   This book has provided an answer to this question. In the first place, Buddhist followers should understand what Buddhism is all about. They may have only some vague ideas, but so long as such ideas are in line with or consistent with the main focus, they are on the right track. They should then adopt a right attitude in what they do. Some authors would refer to the attitude as "the Eight Rightful Paths," "the Four Noble Truths," etc. Master Chin Kung has referred to them, citing from the sutras, as "Truthfulness, purity, equality, the right understanding, and compassion." Moreover, it is important that we see through the true value of things and we are able to abandon our rights and feel comfortable in spite of such abandonment. We must not crave things beyond our reach and must be mindful of what Buddhism has taught us. This has been discussed in Chapter 6.

9. Do Buddhists apply what they learn to what they do?

   It is very important that we must be able to practice what we have learned. The principles of Buddhism have perfect application in guiding our conduct in our daily lives. We have tried to provide our readers with advice in several instances. (See the latter part of Chapter 6 and Chapter 10 explaining how untoward incidents could turn out to be an opportunity for our cultivation.)

10. Why is Buddhism meaningful? How does Buddhism change our way of life?

    These are very important questions. When one understands the big picture of Buddhism, one will not miss this point. If you feel that you still have doubts after having read this book, we suggest that you read it one more time.

22

The Misconception That Buddhism Is Polytheistic

Westerners could just take a look at the sculptures found inside a Buddhist temple, and immediately, they would form the opinion that Buddhism is polytheistic. We have the burden of proof to explain why it is not. Let us examine what we would normally find inside a Buddhist temple. As we enter a typical Buddhist temple, the first hall we pass through is called the Hall of the Heavenly Guardians. Heavenly Guardians are also known as Dharma Protectors. Situated at the center of the hall, facing the front door is Maitreya Bodhisattva.[1] He wears a big smile. This smile is meant to convey the idea that to learn Buddhism, one should learn to be cheerful and courteous to all. He also has a big belly, which represents fairness, flexibility, impartiality, patience, and tolerance in the Chinese culture. Only by possessing these virtues can one become a true Buddhist.

Of the four Dharma Protectors stationed at the four corners—east, south, west, and north—the Eastern Dharma Protector[2] is the Heavenly Guardian designated to assist a leader in taking charge of a territory. When a person is in charge of a family, he or she is the one supporting the family. When one is in charge of company, he or she is a manager or executive official. When one is in charge of a country, one is a king or president. How can one fulfill one's tasks? The person must be responsible and do what he can to safeguard the interests of the territory. What is interesting is that we can see that the Eastern Dharma Protector carries a violin in his hand. This is supposed to teach us always to remember that he must strike a balance when he handles the affairs under his control. The strings in the violin must not be too loose nor should they be too tight. So we are taught that in handling our affairs, we must exercise moderation and not go to extremes.

The Southern Dharma Protector[3] is the Heavenly Guardian of Progress, who teaches us that not only do we have to fulfill our obligations, we must also aim

---

1 弥勒菩萨.
2 东方持国天王.
3 南方增长天王.

at making progress all the time. He carries in his hand a sword, referred to as the sword of wisdom. What it means is that he will cut off all unnecessary troubles bothering our minds.

The Western Dharma Protector[4] teaches us the need to open our eyes and pay attention to things around us. He has a dragon (sometimes a snake) at his disposal to protect him. The dragon is known to be quick to cope with changes. We are taught to appreciate that everything that we see is changing, and we must know how to manage such changes.

Finally, the Northern Dharma Protector[5] teaches us to listen to what we hear. We notice that he carries an umbrella. The idea is to teach us that the purity of the heart needs protection against pollution from outside.

We will now explain the display of sculptures in the main hall of the temple. The central figures comprise three personalities representing the Buddha and two Bodhisattvas. Note that the combination is always one plus two, meaning one predominant figure plus two subordinates.

Buddha represents the true nature of the universe and human life, which is called "Buddha nature." The word *Buddha* is translated from Sanskrit and means someone who is totally enlightened. A Bodhisattva represents a person who has also achieved enlightenment but who has not yet reached the state of Buddhahood in that his mind is still set in motion. The mind of a Bodhisattva continues to work toward helping others get enlightened. Thus, both the Buddha and the Bodhisattva are indications of levels of attainment.

There are four Bodhisattvas to teach us the entirety of Buddhist teachings, namely:

1. Earth Treasure Bodhisattva[6] of Jiuhua Mountain, to teach us filial piety
2. Great Compassion Bodhisattva[7] of Putuo Mountain, to teach us compassion
3. Great Wisdom Bodhisattva[8] of Wutai Mountain, to give us wisdom
4. Universal Worthy Bodhisattva[9] of Emei Mountain, to teach us about the practical application of what we have learned, including filial piety, respect, and compassion in our daily lives

---

4　西方广目天王.
5　北方多闻天王.
6　地藏菩萨.
7　观音菩萨.
8　文殊菩萨.
9　普贤菩萨.

Thus, when we pay respect and bow toward the sculptures, we worship the virtues that those figures represent. We visualize the image of the sculpture as representing the goodness it is meant to represent. Nothing is tangible. It is not a sign of polytheism. So the entirety of Buddhism is covered by the four qualities: *filial piety, compassion, wisdom,* and *practical application* of what we have learned.

Throughout the centuries, Chinese culture has held the notion that the spirit of a person (including those of our ancestors) continues to exist after death. As we are aware, it places heavy emphasis on the importance of filial piety. We are accustomed to setting up an altar (or simply a framed photo of our deceased parents) in our own home (and perhaps burning incense at regular intervals) as a sign of our respect to our ancestors. We must not look at this practice as polytheistic.

People going to temples do ask the Buddha and the Bodhisattvas for help. There is no denial about that. As explained above, the titles of the Buddha and the Bodhisattvas are just names to describe special qualifications. We need to remember always that all Buddhas as well as Bodhisattvas belong to and form part of a group of perfections. Thus we are taught that they are the same in nature.[10] As a class, they are referred to as the One Truth Dharma Realm. It is never an issue who is superior to the others. There is never a divergence of opinion within the One Truth Dharma Realm.

One Truth Dharma Realm

Buddhism has a concept known as the "One Truth Dharma Realm."[11] Briefly, the principle could be explained as follows:

1. Self-nature is innate of all beings including human beings.
2. The self-nature is immaculate, perfect, and all-powerful.
3. We are unable to "appreciate" our self-nature because of our shortcomings. As the Buddha Shakyamuni said, these shortcomings are one's attachments and wandering thoughts, which block us from appreciating our self-nature.
4. The following analysis by the most venerable patriarch Hui-neng, as reported in the Tan Sutra of self-nature, is very relevant.

---

10 诸佛如一.
11 一真法界.

What is expected of self-nature, it is purity by itself,

What is expected of self-nature, it does not begin and it does not end,

What is expected of self-nature, it comprises all that is needed,

What is expected of self-nature, it doesn't move with its surroundings,

What is expected of self-nature, it has the capability of creating everything.[12]

5. Thus, with a true understanding of the self-nature, one should see that the self-nature is capable of creating and did originate all matters in the universe, including the perfect system mentioned in Chapter 1. Everything in the universe is a reflection of the self-nature.

6. If the self-nature, being perfect, has created something, then what it created and the self-nature itself must both be perfect. So, the perfection must be treated as one and not two. The reasoning is this: Suppose someone who is beautiful creates something which is also beautiful; the beauty in either case must be different. They could not be treated as one. Two things might be good or beautiful for different reasons, but if something is perfect, there can only be one perfection, although the perfection could appear in different forms. The One Truth Dharma Realm describes a state of perfection in different forms. It is sometimes referred to as "the Big Perfection."[13] The perfection exists in the self-nature, being one and the same as the nature of the Buddha.

7. A person who gets enlightened becomes a Buddha. We worship the goodness of the Buddha. We may worship Buddha "A" or Buddha "B." Whether we worship the goodness of Buddha "A" or Buddha "B" or for that matter, Guan-yin Bodhisattva does not make any difference. It is the same perfection as covered by the One Truth Dharma Realm.

As we said earlier on, those of us who succeed in completely freeing ourselves from discriminatory and wandering thoughts and attachments, including our fixations with certain ideas or objects, will regain our lost Buddhahood; that is to say, we will restore our self-nature and become true nature Buddhas.

The process of becoming a Bodhisattva is similar except that in the case of Buddhahood, it refers to one who has reached perfection in both self-realization

---

12 何期自性 本自清净；何期自性 本不生灭；何期自性 本自具足；何期自性 本无动摇；何期自性 能生万法。

13 大圆满。

and helping others to reach realization. In the case of Bodhisattvas, it refers to someone who has vowed to attain supreme enlightenment for not just themselves but all beings.

Because of the vast numbers of people wanting to seek help from the Buddha to get rich, it is essential that we explain how the Buddha who is called the goddess of wealth[14] came into being. We begin by explaining how the goddess of wealth, known as Fàn Lí, came about. Fàn Lí was someone who lived during the Era of the Warring Kingdoms. It was said that Fàn Lí possessed the skill of amassing tremendous wealth. He built up a huge fortune for himself. Soon after that, he gave away all he had in helping others and became penniless. He started all over again, and again, he built up a fortune a second time. As on the previous occasion, he gave away all he had. In his lifetime, he succeeded in building up a fortune three times, and three times, he gave away what he had. After his death, people honored him as a goddess of wealth and turned to him (or rather his immortality with a sculpture as his resemblance) for help when money had to be made. There are other Buddhas by different names, and each one is given a Buddhahood for some quality we admire. There is, for this reason, a number of goddesses of wealth!

Let us summarize the way we look at people going to worship the Buddha and the Bodhisattvas:

1. The sculptures we find in a temple or in the homes of Buddhist followers represent a symbol of Buddhahood and/or that of a Bodhisattva. They project the image of the Buddha and/or a Bodhisattva.
2. Neither the Buddha nor the Bodhisattva is treated as a god. Both are symbols of perfection.
3. The concept of the One True Dharma Realm explains that being enlightened, the Buddha and the Bodhisattva fall within the same grouping of perfection. There is oneness in the perfection, and it is not a case of worshipping multiple gods.
4. There is no objection to praying for help from the Buddhas or the Bodhisattvas. Buddhists are taught that their prayers are always answered.

When we read the sutras including the Flower Adornment Sutra, we are convinced that from the very beginning of the introduction of Buddhism, the Buddha had already introduced the concept of the One True Dharma Realm. This principle was introduced and clearly understood from the Buddhist scriptures. Those

---

14 财神.

who read the Chinese translation of the sutras will have the benefit of learning directly the essence of Buddhism from the Buddha's own revelation. Western students learning from textbooks written in English do not appear to have the same luxury.

While we discuss what we find inside a temple, we should appreciate that what we see there often teaches us something. It would be helpful to our cultivation if we could know the meaning behind what we see.

Thus, we often see a small cup containing water being placed in front of the Buddha. Water symbolizes purity. It reminds us of the need for our hearts to be clean like pure water. There is never a storm in the teacup in Buddhism. Our hearts should be as peaceful as the water in the cup.

We offer flowers and fruit to the Buddha. Flowers symbolize the causation of things, and fruit symbolizes the consequence. We are taught to always remember the inevitable relationship between cause and consequence. The lamp close to the image of the Buddha symbolizes light and wisdom. The burning of the candles symbolizes the act of consuming ourselves to brighten up the environment for others.

We can see that there is a meaning in practically everything we find relating to Buddhism. With the explanation set out above, we hope our readers will understand why we say that Buddhism is not polytheistic. The spirit of a person will not die. We pay respect to our ancestors to show filial piety. When a person (whether he was our ancestor or not) set a good example, his spirit deserves our respect. If that person has attained the qualification of a Buddha or a Bodhisattva, we will respect him as such and pray to him for help whenever we think we need help.

We could visualize our relationship with the Buddhas and the Bodhisattvas as that of schoolmates. Anyone who succeeds in his cultivation will be promoted to a relatively senior class in the school. He will work his way toward graduation. The highest ranking of Buddhahood is likened to a graduate student being conferred a doctorate degree. The Bodhisattva status could be compared to a bachelor's degree. Our schoolmates as well as graduates of the school will be in a position to help us, but they are in no position to condemn us and send us to hell. If we have to go to hell, it is the result of our own doings. Similarly, if we were meritorious enough, we would gain a place in heaven. Neither the Buddha nor the Bodhisattvas have any right to decide where to send us upon our demise. This explanation, we hope, will dispel any myths about Buddhism being polytheistic.

How does Buddhism help us to understand ourselves and the circumstances in the universe?

Now that we have an idea of the big picture of Buddhism (as explained in Chapter 2) and now that we know that self-nature has the capability of creating everything we encounter (as explained in Chapter 22) and about the principle of *Yuán Qǐ Fǎ* (as explained in Chapter 10), we can put the jigsaw puzzle together and offer an explanation of the events of the universe and all beings therein.

First, self-nature, being perfect, has brought about a perfect system in which things evolve. According to the *Yuán Qǐ Fǎ*, everything that happens, happens as a result of something. If there was a big crash followed by a big bang, there must be a reason for both scenarios. *Yuán Qǐ Fǎ* must have already played a role. Then when the big bang created the various planets in the universe, *Yuán Qǐ Fǎ* again played a role. From then on, *Yuán Qǐ Fǎ* continued to have a role to play. When different species of creatures lived and disappeared on Earth, the principle of rebirth played a role. It applied even though human beings were not as yet in existence. This principle of rebirth applies today, and it will continue to apply in the future. It will apply to other sentient beings even if one day, all human beings have ceased to exist on Earth.

With this analysis and by looking at things from the Buddhist perspective, we can explain why we are here and why the universe is what it is today.

Part 4

Looking Ahead from the Buddhist Perspective

23

A Look at the Future

Religion and Science

Some writers have suggested that religion is in decline attested by the reduction in the number of people going to church. They talk of disenchantment and secularization. Many believe that the decline is inevitable. It is a phase through which human beings have passed and which they have outgrown. Then, they suggest that the decline is desirable in the sense that in leaving religion behind, we would discard more primitive beliefs and practices and move toward more enlightened ones.[1] In Chapter 1 of this book, I have suggested that "religion" should be redefined. With the new definition, we see that religious beliefs are not necessarily primitive. They do not necessarily clash with science. There is a valid reason for us not to be disenchanted.

Science is nothing more than research on the rules governing the happening of things in the universe, including life on the planet(s). The rules I refer to could be called the rules of nature. In the course of history, we human beings have made many discoveries about these rules. Some of these discoveries are extremely useful in enhancing our quality of life. No doubt further discoveries will continue to be made from time to time. On the future relation between science and religions, we notice that when religious beliefs clash with scientific findings, scientific findings always prevail. Many religious practitioners rely on faith as a basis of their belief. They are naturally concerned that scientific findings might shatter their faith and that of their followers. The relationship between religions and science is sometimes described as "frosty." I firmly believe that this is not a proper attitude with which to look at science and its relationship with religion. We must not put a halt to our research for fear that any findings might contradict our traditional views.

---

1   See Clack, Beverley, and Brian R. Clack. 1998. *The Philosophy of Religion: A Critical Introduction.* Cambridge: Polity Press, p.172 quoting Gordon Graham.

Religion and Harmony

Largely, religions are mildly positive factors in the promotion of peace. I say mildly because all religions teach us to be good and (hopefully) religions do not encourage hatred and conflicts. There is, however, a special reason why we are less optimistic today when we evaluate religion as an institution to promote peace as compared with the situation a few centuries back.

Religions have had a place in politics throughout history. Yet, there is a vast difference between the past and today. The fabric of society has changed dramatically since the introduction of democracy to our political systems. When we talk of democracy in this book, we are referring to a system where once every few years, there will be an election to choose a political party to lead the country.

Prior to this system being introduced, the society was made up of two classes of people: the ruling class and those being ruled. The ruling class would want to use religions to help it reinforce its authority and at the same time promote harmony and stability in the society. Those being ruled were encouraged to follow what was taught.

With the modern system of elections and the prospect of new rulers emerging after an election, there is now a new class of people whom we may refer to as "potential rulers." This new class of people (comprising the members of different political parties) wants to seize power, and it would in all likelihood want to use religion to help it to achieve its goal. A new scenario has developed. Because of this new class of people, our political system has given a new "value" to religions and a new role for religions to play in world affairs.

If religion becomes a means to seize power, it is not too much to say that the high ideals of religiosity are lost. The world is then in trouble, and the problem is not an easy one to deal with. As citizens of the world, we have to take this into account if we want to solve the problem of maintaining peace in different territories around the world.

The Western world wants to introduce democracy to all political systems around the globe. In countries where there exists a population made up of mixed ethnic origins and religious beliefs, it is very likely that those running for power would want to galvanize support from their own religious and ethnic groups. The discontent arising out of the differences in religious and ethnical background would be magnified. Candidates would likely take a rather aggressive stand in criticizing their counterparts from the opposite camps. As a result, preposterous accusations and tricks of all kinds are the rule rather than the exception. Theoretically, competition could still be healthy, but too much is involved. The disappointment of the loser is often so great that animosity and hatred follow.

The problem is therefore not one of a lack of dialogue between different religions nor of different people following different rituals or observing different traditions in distinctive cultures; the problem we face is how to avoid animosity. Political and religious leaders as well as thinkers around the world should investigate how to avoid the animosity created by the rigidity of our political systems and how to prevent religions from being used for ulterior motives. I will not direct our thinking along these lines any further as it is not for a book on Buddhism to comment on the good and bad aspects of politics.

One advantage of dialogues between leaders of different religions is that if they could reach some form of an agreement, they would have a very strong voice. If they could find out the real reason for the suffering the world is facing and then devise a way to remove that suffering, perhaps religious leaders could be a lot more helpful in solving the problems of the world.

Why Buddhist Teachings Are Helpful in Promoting Peace

Most people seem to have the impression that Buddhism is helpful in promoting peace, but we seldom hear anyone explain in more specific terms why Buddhism is so meaningful. In fact, if we understand the core value of Buddhism, the reason is obvious. We can analyze world affairs from a Buddhist perspective and say what went wrong and why it went wrong. What the Buddha taught is just as relevant today as it was 2,500 years ago. Let us analyze the major world events of the last two hundred years from a Buddhist perspective. We list some of these events chronologically:

The Rise of Colonialism Led by Great Britain

The Opium War was a classic example of selfishness. George Elliot must have had this in mind before he opened fire on the Chinese: "If you don't allow what is labeled today as 'drugs' to be freely distributed to your people, I am going to punish you with my gunboats." The motivation was "greed." I mention this not because I want to single out the wrongdoing of a particular government or people; rather, I want to point out that human weakness knows no territorial (or national) boundaries. In the world today, I recommend that we do not look for a reason to blame a particular government or people but rather concentrate our efforts on finding a solution to solve the problems we face.

The Two World Wars—Especially World War II

The benefits (just or unjust) brought about by colonialism prompted the Germans and the Japanese to imitate what the British did. Again, from a Buddhist perspective, this was "greed."

The Mishandling of the Middle East after World War II

Israel was established in 1946. There was nothing wrong with the establishment of Israel. The problem was the failure to establish a similar territory for the Palestinians and a failure to look after their interests. The Buddhist perspective would look upon this as a "differentiation." Buddhists believe in equality. Endless troubles ensued simply because the world powers chose to differentiate between the two peoples.

Domination of Eastern Europe with Communism as an Ideology

The former Soviet Union, in its domination of its satellite countries in Eastern Europe (1946–89), demonstrated a desire to dominate the world with its ideology. Buddhism would look upon this as "greed" and "delusion." As a result of such a desire, an arms race between two superpowers followed, creating an extremely dangerous situation. With the abandonment of such desire, the danger subsided.

Today, if the leader of a certain country has a desire motivated by greed, anger, or delusion to benefit himself, for example by being able to stay in power, or even to benefit his own country, danger will emerge. This danger is especially alarming if this leader happens to head a country with nuclear capability.

Terrorism

What is the frame of mind of terrorists? They might feel that they were aggrieved and they want to avenge what they perceive as a wrong. Alternatively, they might think that they are doing the right and proper thing in causing havoc. In the first case, they are motivated by anger. In the latter case, it is delusion that prompts their actions.

One wonders whether the people around the world could ever abandon greed, hatred, and delusion even for a short duration of time. Unfortunately, unless these three poisons are removed, the world will continue to face the risk of catastrophic destruction of its civilizations.

Another reason why Buddhism is especially helpful in promoting peace and harmony around the world is summarized in the One Unity Perception. We have already discussed this exciting topic in Chapter 18. Buddhism takes the view that we should treat the universe and all beings as one unit. We all are part of that unit. The One Unity Perception has provided us with a good reason not to kill other beings and to protect the environment.

Apart from in Buddhism, it seems that religious teachings have largely remained silent about the reasons for protecting the environment. Scientists now suggest that probably due to our neglect and disrespect of the environment, the clock toward the end of the world has moved faster by two minutes. With this threat hanging over our heads, it is about time that we start to work toward solving the environmental problems. This may be a necessary cooperation forced upon different peoples around the world. Can we succeed? We must try. More important, cooperation will take place when we realize that we have the capacity to work together.

In his book *Buddhism: A Very Short Introduction*, Mr. Damien Keown expresses the need for "a systematic updating of the intellectual foundations of Buddhism so as to allow a clear and consistent set of teachings on the modern issues."[2] The implication is that in his opinion, the intellectual foundations, as he described them, are not as yet in place. If my readers agree with what I said in Chapter 2, Buddhist teachings have clearly provided an answer to the problems of today. The problems will be solved only if we can control our greed, hatred, and delusion.

Religions are never static. The several so-called authentic religions the world recognizes today have been in existence for more than a thousand years. Religions and cultures have influenced each other and will continue to do so.

Throughout history, people in power were accustomed to relying on a certain religion, or their affinity to a religion, to fortify their authority. Probably on this account, religions have played an important role in shaping history. But today, as I have explained, with a system of elections for power called "democracy," the role of religions is much more complicated than what it was in the past. Religions can easily be used as a means to galvanize support for realizing a political ambition. In the process, there is bound to be confrontation. Some people believe that confrontation without the use of violence is healthy and should be encouraged. Others feel that confrontation in whatever form is uncomfortable and dangerous.

It is submitted that being the opposite of harmony, confrontation is destructive. Common sense tells us that if confrontation is not checked, it may lead us toward much more serious consequences. It is foolish for the advanced nations to

---

2   Keown, Damien. 2000. *Buddhism: A Very Short Introduction*. New York: Oxford University Press, p. 123.

underestimate the capability of the underdogs. Human intelligence is unpredictable, and it cannot be suppressed. Confrontation is especially dangerous today when human beings have the knowledge to develop various types of weapons of mass destruction. If hatred persists, based on our knowledge of the inevitable relationship between cause and consequence, we know there will be disasters ahead, but we cannot predict the trigger to such disasters.

How Can the World Receive Buddhism in the Future?

How can the world receive Buddhism in the future? We can consider this from three points of view:

1. *Individuals*

    If one had the opportunity to do an analysis of the reasons for an individual to accept a particular religion, we would find the following factors relevant. A person's acceptance or nonacceptance of a religion depends to a large extent on:

    a. The view of other members of the family or that of friends or other members of the community

    b. The stand of the government, whether it is for or against a particular religion(s)

    c. The consequences from a materialistic point of view of joining or not joining a religion

    d. Our opportunity of exposure to, hence an understanding of, a particular religion

    e. Sometimes, regulatory constraint

    Thus, we can say that the choice of a person has only a limited impact on the spread of a religion. External factors are much more relevant.

    For the future, we can say that it is very likely that Buddhism will be better understood. Many will agree that it stands up to logic. It does not clash with our limited knowledge of evolution and science. Yet, for a thousand and one reasons, the chance of Buddhism taking over the popularity of other religions such as Christianity and Islam is slim.

2. *Other religious institutions*

Whether the principles of a religion are sound does not depend on the percentage of people accepting that religion. Yet, many people take the view that the majority must be right. Probably for this reason, the leaders of some religions are very concerned with their success in recruiting new followers. It is not easy for other religious institutions to accept Buddhism. This stand is not likely to be changed. Both Islam and Roman Catholicism are very specific. The First Commandment has made it abundantly clear: "Thou shall not have strange gods before me." In this regard, Buddhism takes a much more liberal view toward other religions.

Two provisions in the Diamond Sutra deserve our special attention. The first is the revelation found in Section 17 where it says that all dharma is Buddha's Dharma.[3] Buddha's Dharma is also referred to as the Buddha Way. The second is found in the last sentence in Section 8 where it says that when we mention Buddha's Dharma, it is not Buddha's Dharma[4]; it is just so called.

We have already explained in Chapter 6 how any deed could be a Buddha Way. Buddhism does not claim exclusivity of good deeds.

As for the last sentence in Section 8, one way to interpret the provision, as I understand it, is simply this: Strictly speaking, anyone who is enlightened will see that based on Buddhist principles, everything that we come across, including Buddha's Dharma, is unreal and illusory. So Buddha's Dharma is nothing. Yet, to enable those who are not yet enlightened to understand what is good and what is bad, we normally refer to good deeds as "Buddha's Dharma or Buddha's Way." Let's say we use "Buddha's Dharma" to refer to the act of helping others to get enlightened. Without doubt, helping others to get enlightened is meritorious. To describe it as "Buddha's Dharma" seems acceptable. Yet "Buddha's Dharma" is only a term used to refer to good deeds. Good deeds could be known by other names. For example, some good deeds might be called "the route to salvation." We should not be so particular on how an act is labeled. It is the motive that counts. So when we see that the practitioners of some other religions have their own way to teach their followers to do what they think is good, we have every reason not to challenge them by saying that our practice is the Buddha Way and theirs is not. Indeed, "the route to salvation" is also the Buddha's Way. In this sense, Buddhism has

---

3   Referred to as 故如来说：「一切法皆是佛法。」.
4   Referred to as 所谓佛法，即非佛法，是名佛法.

helped us to adopt an attitude of tolerance and peaceful coexistence. It is certainly conducive to bringing harmony in a society having a diversity of religions. Buddhism welcomes competition and deliberation. It does not feel threatened by the success of other religious institutions.

3. *Governments*

Dealing with the acceptance of religious activities in different countries, it seems that governments could be divided into three categories depending on their attitude toward religious activities:

a. The truly secular governments
b. Those governments where politics and religious consideration are intertwined
c. Governments that are neither completely secular nor completely religious but somewhere in between

China belongs to Category (a). It provides for freedom of religious belief. No authentic religion is discriminated against. This is subject to the very important proviso that no institution, or rather no person, can use religion as a means to challenge or even to influence the politics in the country. The sole and exclusive right to the administration of its own domestic affairs is vested with the government, and it cannot be compromised. The government claims that it must have the exclusive right to do what it thinks is best in the promotion of harmony and stability in the country. For example, a foreign entity, such as the Vatican, cannot have the final say in the appointment of a bishop in the country.

Chinese culture places emphasis on harmony. It encourages its people to analyze different points of view to find out the facts.[5] Thus, when being confronted with a new religion like Buddhism from India about two thousand years ago, it did not reject it. And similarly, when Islam was introduced to China, during the ninth century, it also received support. The same was true when Matteo Ricci (1552–1610) introduced Christianity to China in an organized way. Chinese culture does not object to people holding different views, but it has always emphasized that people should live in harmony whilst holding different views.[6]

---

5 Chinese people are taught of the need to 格物致知.
6 This concept is 君子和而不同.

Some critics of China say that Communism is against religions. When did this important principle change? they ask. It appears that the important meeting of December 1978 changed the whole picture when the ruling Communist party decided that the truth could only be ascertained from pragmatic experience. If pragmatic experience shows that the people need religious support, the people must have religious support. So in China today, we are given to understand that religions are allowed and all the important authentic religions receive equal treatment.

Many countries in the Middle East belong to the (b) category. The authorities there will not allow any religious activities other than Islamic ones to be promoted in these countries.

Many Western countries belong to the (c) category. Here, there is freedom of religious beliefs. The people in these countries are predominantly Christians. Yet, although the people living in these countries are free to choose their religions, Christianity is part of their culture; and the authorities are vigorously supporting it. For example, Christianity is made a compulsory subject in the curriculum of primary schools in Great Britain.

In these countries, for example, in Spain and Portugal, the Roman Catholic authorities would gladly accept the appointment of bishops by the head of the Vatican, although one cannot be so sure that they could allow the same for Islam. It is unthinkable that the US government would officially recognize the appointment (from Saudi Arabia or Iran or some other country in the Middle East) of someone to head and develop Islamic movements inside the USA.

What is the likely scenario for the future? Will the different governments be more pronounced in their policies about accepting or not accepting different religions? Will any one or two of the above-mentioned categories totally disappear, or will there be a fourth category? Only time will tell.

Having distinguished between the policies of different governments, let us return to our discussion on the future of Buddhism. Will the modern world accept Buddhism? Some critics say that: (1) Buddhism is superstitious; (2) it is not a religion for the elitists; and (3) the church of Christianity, for example, is seen to provide counseling and consolation to its members when they are in need of such services. Buddhist institutions do not offer assistance of a similar nature.

I am not unduly worried about the allegation that Buddhism is superstitious. There are bound to be rituals in any religion. The practices seemingly superstitious are usually carried out as a result of people following after a tradition. If a practice is not offensive and it is not doing any harm to anybody or to society, it may not be necessary to challenge it. From a personal point of view, it would be ideal if pompous ceremonies with practitioners in colorful attire could be avoided.

On the second point, throughout this book, I have demonstrated that Buddhism is logical and compatible with science. It is peaceful, and it has a noble ideal. It aims at perfection, and it upholds equality. With all these facts in mind, when I look at Buddhism, I feel quite comfortable.

The third point is a real concern. I agree that Buddhist practitioners must do something as an institution to help Buddhism's followers. This topic is sometimes referred to as social engagement. Buddhist practitioners have not done enough. They should learn from the invaluable social services offered by the church. Nonprofit Buddhist organizations with a dedicated commitment to do charity have come to the public's attention. An outstanding example of success was Venerable Master Sheng-yen's organization, Dharma Drum Mountain. This and other organizations with similar aims deserve our highest respect. Perhaps some guidelines could be devised by legislature to give the public incentive to follow after such practices.

For one reason or another, the functions of the temples, especially those in China, have changed substantively in recent years. Many elaborately built temples have become tourist spots, and they are used as a means to enable the practitioners there to earn a living. For the future, these old temples will probably continue to be predominantly used as they are today. It is hoped that new centers will be established. If new centers are to be built, they should be more appropriately described as "centers for religious study." A new era for the promotion of understanding in Buddhism could be introduced. Advanced technology in communication could be used in the study centers to provide televised lectures to the visitors. This will be most helpful in making Buddhism better known. E-books should be available for free download. There is no reason for the hard and fast rule that a person must be a monk or a nun to be qualified to impart the knowledge of Buddhism to the public, as is the current tradition. A new qualification will probably be introduced to enable the teachers specialized in Buddhism to lead an ordinary family life. In establishing these study centers, we should bear in mind that nothing needs to be done to discredit or belittle other religions. It is all a matter of understanding the truth. Understanding does not start with hostility.

To enable all this to happen, whether in China or in other regions, it is essential that the people have a better understanding of Buddhism as a first step. This is exactly what this book wants to achieve.

Appendix

I was invited to attend an international forum organized by UNESCO and cosponsored by the Indonesian government held in Bali from January 21–23, 2007. The topic for discussion was the relationship between religion, media, and peace. I talked about the application of the principle of the Four Noble Truths to handle the problems of today. The following is an excerpt from this speech.

A Presentation on the Role of Religions in Conflict and Peace at the Global Forum on Religion, Media, and Peace: "Building Peace through Communication and Information"

Ladies and Gentlemen,

The subject matter of our discussion today deals with three things: religion, media, and peace. The big question is, is religion a positive or negative force for peace? And what could the media do to help to promote peace? I will deal with both of these issues.

In my view, *religion* is neutral. A lot depends on how people handle issues involving religion. The political systems that human beings have designed are also very relevant. I say this because by and large, in any election in a territory involving ethnic and religious diversity, if I am an Orthodox Christian, I would want to support a candidate holding the same faith. The same is true for Muslims wanting a Muslim candidate. At the end, the society is prone to be divided along the lines of religious diversity. This appears to be the situation in Chechnya. Bosnia, Iraq today, and Rwanda, etc., are similar under different circumstances.

Nobody can deny that the world is full of hatred. Nobody seems to have a solution. Usually, the interested parties like to put the blame on their opponents.

I recommend that we should not insist on saying who is right and who is wrong. As soon as we attempt to do so, we are running farther and farther away from finding a solution.

What I'd like to suggest is that we should take a new approach. I suggest that we should make use of certain wisdom of religion developed some 2,500 years ago to solve the problems of today. The wisdom I refer to is the concept of the

Four Noble Truths in Buddhism. I am not trying to promote Buddhism here. The concept of the Four Noble Truths is simply that in times of suffering, we should take a four-step approach:

1. We need to truly identify what our suffering is;
2. We need to find out why we have to face this suffering;
3. We should then take steps to put an end to the suffering; and finally,
4. We must find the correct way to do so.

There is not a shadow of doubt that almost everybody in the Middle East is suffering because of the hostilities there during the past several decades. Adopting the Four Noble Truths approach, simple as it may sound, is pragmatic and is exactly what we should do to solve the problems there, as it is anywhere else.

To use this approach, there must be an appropriate conduit for dialogues on a multilateral level. In the course of such dialogues, we shall be able to identify that there are some ideas that will receive unanimous support. There are also some ideas that will not. We should work on developing those ideas that have unanimous support. Adopting this approach will magnify the agreement we can reach and minimize the significance of any disagreements obstructing the path of peace. With this strategy, an atmosphere of harmony will be built. As harmony grows, animosity will retreat.

When I talk of dialogues between different religions, I do not mean to confine myself to dialogues between the leaders of different religions. It is ideal if they can come forward. Unfortunately, a person representing a branch of a religion may not find it appropriate to claim, nor has he the authority, to represent all the branches of the religion. On this account, there may be a problem if we confine ourselves to seeking only their views. Multilateral dialogue is perhaps the only way to ascertain the views of the majority of the people.

The media could seek the views of a vast number of individual followers as representatives of different religions. Multilateral cooperation could then be secured. Modern technology has made it possible for the media to do this job.

On the next question, what else could the media do to promote peace? The one advantage of media doing this job is that it has no political boundary. It does not represent any particular country. On this account, the media is exceptionally powerful. Neutrality is a core value of reporting. But instead of just reporting, I think the media should consider doing what it can to achieve the following four objectives:

1. It should try to change the attitude of people in helping them to remove greed, hatred, and ignorance—the major causes of all conflicts.
2. It should try to make people around the world understand the goodness of religions, indeed, of all religions.
3. Do what it can to make sure that governments understand the need to relieve poverty, and
4. Do what it can to ensure that the political systems of the world do not generate confrontation and hatred. We are all against authoritarian governments. Can we have the ideals of democracy without explosive confrontation?

Glossary

Affliction (烦恼 *Fannao*) A condition or cause of pain, distress, and suffering which disturbs the body and mind.

Amitabha (阿弥陀 *Amituo*) The name of the Buddha of the Western Pure Land, primarily meaning Infinite Life and Infinite Light.

Amitabha Sutra (佛說阿弥陀經 *Amituo Jing*) The principle sutra used in the Pure Land School of Buddhism.

Arhat (阿罗汉 *Alouhan*) the Chinese transliteration of the Sanskrit arhat, the name for those who achieve the highest realm of spiritual attainment in the practices of the so-called Hinayana tradition of Buddhism. Once this realm is reached, all vexation ceases, and one is released from the cycle of rebirth and enters nirvana.

Attachment (执着 *Zhizhuo*) Fixed to certain ideas or objects.

Bodhi Resolve or Bodhi Mind (菩提心 *Puti Xin*) The great compassionate and sincere mind, with every thought to attain complete self-realization for self and others.

Bodhisattva (菩萨 *Pusa*) One who has vowed to attain supreme enlightenment for themselves and all beings.

Buddha (佛 *Fo*) One who has reached perfection in both self-realization and helping others to reach realization.

Buddha Nature (佛性 *Fo Xing*) The nature of perfection, same as self-nature.

Buddha Speaks of the Infinite Life Sutra of Adornment, Purity, Equality, and Enlightenment (佛說无量寿经 *Fo Shuo Wuliang Shou Jing*) known also as the Infinite Life Sutra.

Chan School (禅宗 *Chan Zong*) A school of thought to explain and to teach Buddhism.

Cultivation (修行 *Xiu Xing*) Putting the Buddha's teachings into practice on a continuous and regular basis.

Delusion (迷惑 *Mi Huo*) False beliefs and views.

Dharma (法 *Fa*) Sometimes capitalized in English, 1) the teachings of the Buddha; 2) things, events, phenomena, everything in the universe; and 3) duty, law, and doctrine.

Dharma Flower (Lotus) Sutra (法华经 *Fahua Jing*) The principle sutra used in the Tiantai School of Buddhism.

Earth Treasure Sutra (地藏经 *Dicang Jing*) This sutra explains how Earth Store Bodhisattva attained his position among the greatest Bodhisattvas as the Foremost in Vows. It also explains the workings of karma, how beings undergo rebirth, and the various kinds of heavens and hells.

Five Pure Land Sutras and One Treatise (净土五经一论 *Jingtu Wujing Yi Lun*) (1) The Buddha Speaks of the Infinite Life Sutra of Adornment, Purity, Equality, and Enlightenment of the Mahayana School (The Infinite Life Sutra); (2) the Amitabha Sutra; (3) the Visualization on the Infinite Life Buddha Sutra; (4) "Universal Worthy Bodhisattva's Conduct and Vows," from the Flower Adornment Sutra; (5) "The Chapter on the Perfect Complete Realization of Great Strength Bodhisattva through Buddha Name Recitation" from the Surangama Sutra; and (6) the Rebirth Treatise.

Flower Adornment Sutra (华严经 *Huayan Jing*) A very important sutra used as the main guideline for the Huayan School of Thought in Buddhism.

Good Fortune (福报 *Fu Bao*) Happiness, intelligence, well-being, prosperity, etc. The great benefits of the human and celestial realms, they are temporary and subject to birth and death.

Hinayana (or Hinayanan Buddhism) See Theravada Buddhism below.

Infinite Life Sutra (无量寿经 *Wuliang Shou Jing*) See Buddha Speaks of the Infinite Life Sutra of Adornment, Purity, Equality, and Enlightenment.

Karma/Cause and Effect (业 *Ye* 因果 *Yin Guo*) Consequences result from thought, speech, and behavior. Karma mainly applies to intentional thoughts.

Mahayana (大乘 *Da Cheng*) One of the two major branches of Buddhism, it is the Bodhisattva path of helping all sentient beings to attain enlightenment.

Maitreya Bodhisattva (弥勒菩萨 *Milei Pusa*) The Bodhisattva to convey the first impression to a newcomer wanting to learn Buddhism.

Merits and Virtues (功德 *Gong De*) They are accumulated by doing good deeds selflessly without expectation of reward and without wandering or discriminatory thoughts or attachments.

Phenomena (事相 *Shi Xiang*) Things, events, happenings—everything in the entire universe.

Precepts (戒 *Jie*) Rules that were set up by Buddha Shakyamuni to guide his students from erroneous thoughts, speech, and behavior.

Pure Mind or Purity of Mind (清净心 *Qingjing Xin*) The mind without wandering and discriminatory thoughts and attachments.

Refuge (皈依 *Gui Yi*) A return to relying on three qualities referred to as the Three Gems including the Buddha, the precepts, and the monks. It is within the qualities of these objects that one should seek refuge; namely, Buddha represents enlightenment, the precepts represent correctness, and the monks represent purity.

Retribution (报应 *Bao Ying*) Karmic punishment for erroneous thoughts, words, or deeds.

Sangha (僧团 *Seng Tuan*) A group of four or more people who properly practice the Buddha's teachings together, especially the Six Harmonies.

Self-nature (自性 *Zi Xing*) A perfect nature originally vested in man, which is blocked by shortcomings including greed, hatred, and delusion. Self-nature is equivalent to Buddha Nature.

Sentient being (众生 *Zhong Sheng*) A living being that is self-aware and that can experience feeling or sensation.

Six Harmonies (六和敬 *Liu He Jing*) Buddhist concept of how people should treat others in their joint cultivation for merits.

Six Paramitas (六度 *Liu Du*) Giving (布施 *Bu Shi*), self-discipline (持戒 *Chi Jie*), patience (忍辱 *Ren Ru*), diligence (精进 *Jing Jin*), deep concentration (禅定 *Chan Ding*), and wisdom (智能 *Zhi Hui*).

Six Realms (六道 *Liu Dao*) The three upper realms are heavens, asuras, and humans. The three lower realms are animals, hungry ghosts, and hells.

Six Senses (六境 *Liu Jing*) Sight (色 *Se*), hearing (声 *Shen*), smell (香 *Xiang*), taste (味 *Wei*), touch (触 *Chu*), and thought (法 *Fa*). External.

Sutra (经 *Jing*) Teaching by the Buddha, initially given verbally, later compiled and written down by the Buddha's students.

Ten Virtuous Conducts (十善业 *Shi Shan Yie*) No killing (不杀生 *Bu Sha Sheng*), stealing (不偷盗 *Bu Todao*), sexual misconduct (不邪淫 *Bu Xieyin*), lying (不妄语 *Bu Wangyu*), abusive language (不恶口 *Bu E Kou*), bearing tales (不两舌 *Bu Liangshe*), seductive words (不绮语 *Bu Qiyu*), greed (不贪 *Bu Tan*), anger (不瞋 *Bu Chen*), and ignorance (不痴 *Bu Chi*).

Ten Great Vows of Universal Worthy Bodhisattva (普贤十大愿 *Puxian Shi Da Yuan*) 1) Equally respect all beings and things. 2) Praise the virtues and kindnesses of others. 3) Make offerings extensively and respectfully. 4) Feel deep remorse for our faults that obstruct us from seeing our True Nature and vow not to repeat them. 5) Rejoice in every virtuous deed and do not harbor jealousy or hinder others. 6) Request those who truly practice to widely propagate the teachings. 7) Ask teachers to remain in the world and to guide us. 8) Tirelessly uphold the Buddha's teachings in our every thought, word, and deed. 9) Accord with those who are proper and patiently waiting for the opportunity that allows them to guide those who are not. 10) Dedicate the peace and happiness gained from practicing the above deeds to all living beings, hoping that they will attain the unsurpassed understanding.

Theravada Buddhism (小乘 *Xiao Cheng*) The path of strictly abiding by the precepts. The objective is to attain realization for oneself. It is often called the path of the elders and is primarily practiced in Southern Asia and the West. In this book, the term Theravada is loosely used to include Hinayana Buddhism.

Three Blessings (sometimes referred to as the Three Conditions) (三福 *San Fu*) The first blessing is to: (i) Be filial to one's parents, (ii) Be respectful to one's teachers and elders, (iii) Be compassionate and do not kill any living beings, and (iv) Follow the Ten Virtuous Conducts. The second blessing is to: (i) Take the Three Refuges, (ii) Abide by the precepts, laws, and customs, and (iii) Conduct oneself in a proper and dignified manner. The third blessing is to: (i) Give rise to the Bodhi mind, (ii) Firmly believe in the Law of Cause and Effect and that chanting "Amituofo" is the cause and attaining Buddhahood is the effect, (iii) Recite and uphold Mahayana sutras, and (iv) Encourage others to advance on the path to enlightenment.

Three Karmas (三业 *San Ye*) Created by our body (身 *Shen*), mouth (口 *Kou*), and mind (意 *Yi*).

Three Learnings (三学 *San Xue*) Self-discipline, deep concentration, and wisdom.

True Nature (自性 *Zi Xing*) Also called the self-nature, our original, true self that we still have, but that is currently covered by deluded thoughts.

Twelve Causes and Consequences (十二因緣 *Shier Yinyuan*) This is the Buddhist explanation of how life and death came about.

Wandering Discriminatory Thoughts and Attachments (妄想分别执着 *Wangxiang Fenbie Zhizhuo*) Afflictions that cloud our True Nature. When we have no wandering thoughts, we only have absolutely proper and virtuous thoughts. It does not mean that our minds are empty of all thoughts.

Way Place (道场 *Dao Chang*) Usually called a temple, a place where Buddhist practitioners come to practice.

Western Pure Land (极乐世界 *Jile Shijie*) The world created by Buddha Amitabha, which is an ideal place for cultivation; for those who stay there are no longer subject to reincarnation.

Yuán Qǐ Fǎ (缘起法 *Yuan Qi Fa*) It is a concept in Buddhism that whatever we encounter would not have happened without a cause. Nothing comes by chance.

About the Author

Mr. Edward P.H. Woo was born in 1937. He received his education in Hong Kong before proceeding to London to attend law school. Upon his return to Hong Kong in 1962, he started to practice as a solicitor.

In 1969, together with a group of friends interested in finance, Mr. Woo set up the Far East Stock Exchange in Hong Kong. Mr. Woo was also one of the founders of the Commodity Exchange of Hong Kong, serving on the board of the founder company. With his experience in futures trading, Mr. Woo wrote a book entitled *The Winning Art and Logic of Speculation in the Futures Markets*. For many years, Mr. Woo served on the committee of the Far East Stock Exchange and subsequently at the United Stock Exchange of Hong Kong.

In 1979, with another group of friends interested in the promotion of higher education, Mr. Woo set up a private university in Macau called the University of East Asia. The university was converted into a publicly funded university in 1990, and its name was changed to the University of Macau. In 1992, he became involved with the setting up of the Asia International Open University in Macau. He served as the chairman of the administrative council of this university until March 2001, when he retired from that post. He has since continued to serve as the chairman of its consultative council, in addition to acting as the director in charge of the Center of Cantonese Studies.

In the field of education, Mr. Woo invented a system simplifying the process of teaching and learning Cantonese called the "Musical approach." Eventually, this system developed into a discovery about the commonality in the tones of different languages spoken around the world. The discovery is known as the "Theory of the Hexatave."

Mr. Woo was conferred an honorary doctorate in philosophy by the IMC of London.

Mr. Woo has a dedicated interest in looking for improvement to the ways and means of implementing the ideals of democracy. His latest book on politics is called *In Search of an Ideal Political Order & An Understanding of Different Political Cultures*.

Mr. Woo is spending part of his time in Kuala Lumpur.

Index

A
afterlife, 22–23, 26
Agama Sutra, 98
Amitabha Sutra (ā mí tuó jīng), 50
Avici Hell, 22, 23

B
Bhikkhu, Buddhadasa, 83
big bang theory, 21, 90
Big Eight Appreciations Sutra (bā dà rén jué jīng), 52–54, 88–89
Big Learning, The (大学), 69
"Big Perfection, the," 115
Big Sun Sutra, 104
Black Sect Tantric Buddhists, 104
Blessing of Heaven and Man, 41–42, 91
Blessing of the Big Carriage, 43–45
Blessing of the Second Carriage, 42–43
Bodhi Resolve, 35, 44
    compassion and, 92
    perfection in, 99
    selflessness, principles of, 43, 72
    merits, transfer of, 72
Bodhisattva, 33
    Big Eight Appreciations Sutra, 33, 52–54
    entirety of Buddhist teachings, 113
    and giving away, 92
    Maitreya Bodhisattva, 112
    process of becoming, 115–116
    Ten Great Vows of, 70–73
Buddha. *See also* Bodhisattva
    advice of, 49
    answer to prayers, 35–37
    death of, 97
    enlightenment of, 11
    five precepts taught by, 43
    meaning of term, 71, 113
    praise to, 71
    religious teachings, 20–21
Buddha Conservation Sutra, 44, 97
Buddha Dharma, 39, 127. *See also* dharma
Buddhahood, 22, 70, 98, 113, 117. *See also* enlightenment
"Buddha nature," 113
"Buddha Way," 39, 40, 127
Buddhism. *See also* Buddhist philosophy
    afterlife, philosophy of, 9
    basic principle of, 108–109
    belief in, 75
    benefit of learning, xvi
    "cause and consequence" relationship, 13–15, 29
    changes in, 110
    Chinese government, promotion of, 130
    Christianity, comparison with,

16–24
    compassion, importance of, 24
    confusion about, 100
    contemporary books in English, xiv
    core teaching of, xvi
    creation beliefs, 17–18
    culprits, dealing with, 64–65
    design and evolution, concept of, 21, 34
    entirety of, 113–114
    "Four Noble Truths," 12
    future of, 126–130
    love for environment, 91
    peace and harmony, promotion of, 37–38, 123. *See also* One Unity Perception
    perfection, 22
    polytheistic misconception, 112–117
    problems in promotion of, 95–96
    promotion of, 7–8, 128–129
    qualifications to be a Buddhist, 110–111
    questions about, 108–111
    rules and regulations. *See* precepts
    schools of thought, 101
    self-nature, 10–13
    suffering, elimination of, 34–35
    superstitious nature of, 129–130
    symbols, 117
    three poisons, 37
Buddhism: A Very Short Introduction (Keown), 125

Buddhist monks, xv, 50, 83, 104
Buddhist philosophy
    afterlife, 22
    contentment, 35
    promoting, 72
    route to enlightenment, 13
    self-nature, 10–11
Buddhist practitioners, 97
    immoral and corrupt, 103
    social engagement, 130
Buddhist teachings
    criticism, 14, 21
    dealing with truth, 82, 83
    destination, 107
    diligence in, 72
    emptiness, 81
    event, happening of, 63
    peace, promotion of, 123
    self-nature, restoration of, 12
Buddhist temples, 112–113, 130

C
"cause and consequence" relationship, xvi, 13–14, 29
cause and effect, 19. *See also* karma
chán dìn, defined, 68. *See also* concentration
China
    religions, authentication of, 7, 128
    Buddhism, promotion of, 130
    Communist party, 129
    Cultural Revolution (1966–1976), 32
    Islam and Christianity, introduction of, 128
    People's Consultative Council, 64
Chinese Communist Party, 32

Chinese culture
    Buddhist temples, 130
    Communism, 124, 129
    harmony, 128
    meditation, 69
    monarchy, 103
    polytheistic, 114
    "three teachings," 9
Chinese society, and Buddhism, 57
Chin Kung, Master
    calligraphy of, x, 5
    Development of Benevolence without Attachment, The, xiv
    lectures of, 64, xiv, xv
    sutras, purpose of learning, 49
    Understanding Buddhism, 77
Christianity
    creation beliefs, 16–17
    Fifth Commandment, 91
    hell concept in, 22
    love, importance of, 24
    perfection, 22
    Ten Commandments, 40
    in Western countries, 129
code of conduct, xvi, 24, 39–40
colonialism, British, 123
Communism, 124, 129
concentration
    meditational, 68
    as part of Six Paramitas, 68–69
    as part of Three Linkages, 77–78
confrontation, effect of, 125–126
Confucianism, 7, 9
Confucius' teachings, 6
conscience, 3
creation beliefs
    in Buddhism, 17–18
    in Christianity, 16–17
criticism
    of Buddhist teaching, 14, 21
    verbal, 80
Cudworth, Ralph, 20
culprits, dealing with, 35, 64–65
cultivation, practice of, 33
    four stages of, 75–76
    recommendations (or rules), 79. *See also* precepts
    ultimate aim of, 48
Cultural Revolution (China, 1966–1976), 32

D

Dalai Lama
    Yellow Sect, 104
    view on happiness, 12
Darwin, Charles, 21
Dà Xī ng Shàn Sì, Shanxi Province (China), 104
delusion
    blockage of self-nature, 10, 12
    caused by terrorism, 58
    desire motivated by, 124
    elimination of, 37, 58
democracy, 37, 122
"Dependent Origination," 62
desire
    as cause of danger, 124
    selfless, 44, 98
    willingness, 106
destiny, 29, 63
Development of Benevolence without Attachment, The, xiv
dharma, 87–88
    in Diamond Sutra, 82
    emptiness related to, 81
    mind and, 60

taking refuge in, 43
Dharma Drum Mountain, 130
Dharma Flower Sutra. *See* Lotus Sutra
(fǎ huā jīng)
Dharma Protectors
    Eastern Dharma Protector, 112
    Northern Dharma Protector, 113
    Southern Dharma Protector, 112–113
    Western Dharma Protector, 113
Dharma Wheel, 72
Diamond Sutra (jīn gāng bō rě bō luó mì jīng), xv, 39, 51
    dharma and events in, 82, 87
    emptiness in, 83
    One Unity Perception, concept of, 91
"differentiation," 124
"disenchantment," 21
doubt (uncertainity), 3

E

Earth Treasure Sutra (dì zàng jīng), 50, 113
Eastern Dharma Protector, 112
Eight Rightful Paths, xvii, 59–61
Eight Virtues of human beings, 6
Einstein, Albert, 20
Elliot, George, 123
emptiness. *See also* sunnata
    defined, 81
    different views on, 84
enlightenment, 10
    achievement of, 14, 58
    of Buddha, 11
    enlightened *vs.* common, 82
    importance of, 57
    removal of suffering, 12
    and self-nature, 33–34
equality, 124, 130
Esoteric School of Thought (Mì zōng), 49, 104

F

Fàn Lí, 116
Flower Adornment Sutra (huā yán jīng), 11, 51
    four stages in, 75–76
    Great Perfection and, 23
    in Hua Yan School of Thought, 104
Four Grand Wishes, 98
Four Noble Truths, xvii, 56–58
    self-nature, restoration of, 12
    Third, 99. *See also* nirvana
Four Stages, monitoring achievement, xvii, 75–76
Fourteen Lessons of Buddhism, The (Chin Kung) 65
fó yí jiāo jīng sutra, 49

G

giving away
    form of, 35, 48
    practicing of, 64, 71
    types of, 67
God, the creator
    logical proposition about, 3
    as Supreme Being, 4
    in Western consciousness, 4
"Golden Cicada Sheds Its Shell, The," 104
governments
    Buddhism and, 129–130
    religious activities of, 128

and support for Theravada
tradition, 97, 100
"gradual appreciation," 39
Great Compassion Bodhisattva, 113
Great Perfection, 23, 49
Great Wisdom Bodhisattva, 113

H
Hall of the Heavenly Guardians, 112
happiness
    major source of, 12
    practice of, 80
Heart Sutra. *See* Vajra Prajna Paramita Sutra (xīn jīng)
Hua Yan School of Thought (Huā yán zōng), 51, 104–105
Hui-neng, sixth patriarch, 39, 66

I
ignorance. *See* delusion
"initiating cause," 62
Islam
    introduction in China, 128
    promotion of, 129
Israel, establishment of, 124

J
Jammer, Max, 19

K
karma, 48
karmic obstacles, 71
Keown, Damien, 125
kung fu, 102

L
liberation. *See* nirvana
Lin Jia Sutra, 62
London, Scott, 13

Lotus Sutra (fǎ huā jīng), 51
love, importance of, 24

M
Mahayana Buddhism, 44–45
    goal of, 98. *See also* perfection Theravada Buddhism,
comparison with, 97–99, 109
Maitreya Bodhisattva, 112
martial arts, 102
meditation, 68. *See also* concentration
merits, transfer of, 72–73. *See also* Bodhi Resolve
Middle East, 124, 129
Middle Way, 60–61
mind. *See also* concentration; self-nature
    in determining and evaluating objects, 60
    purity of, 43
    as source of evil, 61
morality, 22–23

N
"Navayana," 100
nirvana, 13
    meaning of, 88
    and rebirth, 99
Nirvana Sutra (niè pán jīng), 51, 88
Northern Dharma Protector, 113

O
OALECD. *See* Oxford Advanced Learner's English-Chinese Dictionary (OALECD)
offerings, 71. *See also* giving away
oneness, 90–91
One Truth Dharma Realm, 114–116
One Unity Perception, xvii, 37, 90–92

Opium War, 123
Original Vow of Earth Treasure Bodhisattva Sutra. *See* Earth Treasure Sutra (dì zàng jī ng)
Oxford Advanced Learner's English-Chinese Dictionary (OALECD)
    Buddhism, description of, 5
    philosophy, definition of, 6
    religion, defintion of, 4

P
patience, 68
peace, promotion of, 37–38, 91, 123. *See also* One Unity Perception
precepts, 43, 77
People's Consultative Council, China, 64
Perfect Enlightenment Sutra (yuán jué jī ng), 11
perfection, 14, 22
    aim for, 16
    different forms of, 115
    in self-realization, 115–116
philosophy. *See also* Buddhist philosophy
    afterlife, 9
    defined by OALECD, 6
    versus religion, 6–8
Platform Sutra (Tan Sutra), 68
politics, influence of religion, 122–123
"potential rulers," defined, 122
prayers
    answered by Buddha, 35–37
    for help, 33
Pure Land School of Thought (Jìng tǔ zōng), 50, 105–106
purity, of mind, 88, 105. *See also* Three Blessings of Tranquility

Q
Qianlong (Emperor), xiii
Qianlong Great Buddhist Canon, xiii–xiv

R
rebirth, 9, 13–14, 19
    human race, elimination of, 23
    and nirvana, 99
    and suffering, xvi, 56
refuge in Buddhism, 43
religion
    authenticity of, 125
    choice of acceptance, 126
    definition of, 4–5, 7
    environmental problems, dealing with, 125
    existence of God, 5
    and harmony, 122–123
    need for, 3
    versus philosophy, 6–8
    religious belief, promotion of, 8
    role in shaping history, 125
    science and, 121
    as teaching, 5
    type of, 7
religious beliefs, 75, 110
    freedom of, 128, 129
    promotion of, 8
religious institutions
    Buddhism and, 127–128
    claiming authority by, 49
Ricci, Matteo, 128
right action, 59, 76
right effort, 59

right livelihood, 59
right meditation, 59
right mindfulness, 59
right resolve, 59
right speech, 59
right understanding, 59
"route to salvation, the," 127

S
Saint-Hilaire, 11
schools of thought, 101, 109
    classification of, 102
    Esoteric School, 104
    Hua Yan School, 104–105
    Pure Land School, 105–106
    Tian Tai School, 103–104
science, and religion, 121
scientists, view on
    creation and age of universe, 21
    environmental problems, 125
scriptures, 113, 114. *See also* sutras
self, Buddhist concept of, 87–88
self-defense (martial arts), 102
self-discipline. *See* precepts
selflessness, 43, 89
self-nature. *See also* One Unity Perception
    benefit of learning, 33–34
    blockage of, 10
    Buddhism, 23
    creation beliefs and, 18
    and dharma, 87–88
    nirvana and, 13
    restoration of, 11
self-realization, 115
Shakyamuni. *See* Buddha
Sheng-yen, Master, 130
Shih Jing Yin, 63

singularity (oneness), 90–91
Six Harmonies, 79–80
Six Paramitas, xvii, 46, 67–69
six realms, 22, 100
skepticism, about Buddhism, 95–96
Smart, Ninian
    Buddhist teachings and, 13
    definition of religion, 5
Smith, Huston, 99
"soul", meaning of, 87
Southern Dharma Protector, 112–113
Soviet Union, 124
Spinoza, Baruch, 19
standard of living, 47
"sudden appreciation," 39
Sū Dōng-pō, 40
suffering
    cause of, 57–58
    cessation of, 59
    elimination of, 12, 34–35. *See also* enlightenment
    in hell, 23
    various types of, 56
sunnata, 83
supernatural, 4
sustaining cause, 63, 87
sutras, xiii, 50–51
    Chinese language, translations of, xiv, 50, 117
    purpose of learning, 49
    reciting of, 78
    as reference materials, 104
    written text of, 72

T
Tang Dynasty, xv
Táng Tài Zōng (Emperor), xiii
Táng Xuán Zhung, 50
Tan Sutra (Platform Sutra), 68

Tantric Buddhists, Black Sect, 104
Taoism, 7, 9, 109
Ten Good Deeds Methods Sutra (shí dà shàn yè jīng), 50
Ten Great Vows of Universal Worthy Bodhisattva, 70–73
    in solving real-life problems, 73–74
"Ten thousand dharma, one mind," 60
terrorism, 58, 124
Theravada Buddhism, 44–45
    basic foundation of, 97
    emptiness in, 83
    government support for, 97, 100
    Mahayana Buddhism, comparison with, 97–99, 109
Three Blessings of Tranquility, 40
    Blessing of Heaven and Man, 41–42, 91
    Blessing of the Big Carriage, 43–45
    Blessing of the Second Carriage, 42–43
Three Learnings. *See* Three Linkages
Three Linkages, xvii, 77–78
Three Markings, xvii, 86–89
Three Marks of Existence. *See* Three Markings
three poisons, 37
Three Seals of Dharma. *See* Three Markings
"three teachings," 9
Tian Tai School of Thought (Tiān tái zōng), 51, 103–104
tranquility. *See* Three Blessings of Tranquility
translation, of Buddhist sutras, 50, 1117

"triggering cause," 29, 30, 63
Triple Jewels, 43
"true revelation," 82, 83
T'sing Dynasty, xiii
Twelve Related Causes, 65

U

uncertainty (doubt), 3
understanding, concept of, 75–76
Understanding Buddhism (Chin Kung), 77
universe, creation of, 16–17, 21

V

Vajra Prajna Paramita Sutra (xīn jīng), 51
Vajrayana tradition, 104
verification, importnace of, 76
Visualization Sutra (*Guān Wú Liàng Shòu Jīng*), 40, 50, 79
voidness. *See* emptiness

W

Western Dharma Protector, 113
Western World of Supreme Happiness, 22, 99, 105
willingness, 106
wisdom
    as part of Six Paramita, 69
    restoration of, 34
    story about, 36–37
    in Three Linkages, 77
Wu Ze-tian (Empress), 39

Y

Yellow Sect, 104
YQF. *See* Yuán Qǐ Fǎ (YQF)
Yuán Liao-fán, 30
Yuán Qǐ Fǎ (YQF), xvii, 17, 21

Z

Zen School of Buddhism, 68
zhēn rú zì xìng, 49
Zhìyǐ (Buddhist scholar), 103–104
Zhong Yin-Jin sutra, 14
Zhou Dynasty, 39
Zhōu Wǔ-dì (King), 103